Driving MORE Sales
12 Essential Elements

Patricia Watkins & Dan Doster

Driving More Sales
12 Essential Elements

Patricia Watkins & Dan Doster

FIRST EDITION

ISBN: 978-0-692-95015-9
eBook ISBN: 978-0-692-95065-4

Library of Congress Control Number: 2017954741

Silicon Valley Press

Contents

Introduction

Sales has evolved rapidly with the advent of the Internet, digital tools, social media, and mobile marketing. But these advancements have more often reinforced the basics, rather than replaced them.

We have experience in driving sales across many industries and companies. From start-ups to Fortune 500 companies, we've harnessed best practices, including the latest digital tools across sales, marketing, alliances, and channels. In serving as CEOs, COOs, and vice presidents of sales and marketing, we've learned what works and what doesn't in the Internet age. We both love challenges and significantly creating or changing the landscape to drive positive outcomes. We both have a passion for finding ways to substantially increase sales, and we both have solid track records of results.

Over time, we've developed a sales framework that we've used successfully no matter where we've been and no matter the size of the challenges demanded. Our framework is designed to drive more sales. We call it the "MORE Sales Framework." The MORE Sales Framework links the 12 elements in the MORE diagram below. Harnessing even one of these elements correctly can have a profound impact on driving MORE sales! Harnessing all 12 elements creates a hurricane of effective energy. But before we dig into the details and case studies, here are a few words on each element to provide context and sequence.

M.O.R.E. Sales Framework ™

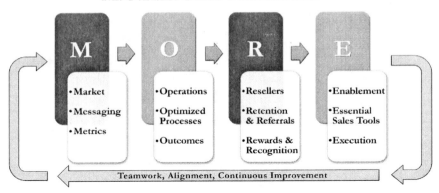

M	O	R	E
•Market	•Operations	•Resellers	•Enablement
•Messaging	•Optimized Processes	•Retention & Referrals	•Essential Sales Tools
•Metrics	•Outcomes	•Rewards & Recognition	•Execution

Teamwork, Alignment, Continuous Improvement

Market

Let's start with the "M" in MORE: A clearly defined *market* is the first step towards successfully orienting the sales process. The selected market must identify a customer segment that needs—and can utilize—the product or service you offer. That's where leveraging your competitive advantages provides the greatest impact and earnings potential.

Messaging

Without a succinct *message* to communicate your offering, and its value, how will prospects know what problem it solves? A compelling message can be driven across all of your market's meaningful channels, not just traditional methods like websites, print, and media advertising. Digital marketing, mobile, and social media should be harnessed as well.

Metrics

Every company collects data. But too few define, capture, and collect data that's useful in driving the desired behaviors. How else can management track the success of its practices without regular meaningful *metrics* to confirm course and speed?

Operations

The "O" in the MORE Sales Framework starts with *operations*. To make salespeople more effective, keep them selling. Offload to others the critical but burdensome administrative and logistical tasks from credit checks to revenue recognition and contracts, to placing and tracking orders, to preparing and maintaining reports and dashboards.

Optimized Sales Processes

It's equally important to *optimize sales processes*. Otherwise, you'll bog down your sales resources and reduce their productivity. Optimized sales processes increase sales velocity and shorten sales cycles.

Outcomes

The ultimate objective is achieving positive *outcomes* for your customers. Focusing on what the customer hopes to achieve closes more sales and sets the stage for glowing referrals.

Resellers/Channel Partners

The "R" element of the MORE Sales Framework starts with *resellers and channel partners*. Both are sales force multipliers. Partners expand your sales capability with additional feet-on-the-street and increased market exposure. The best partners bring trusted relationships with prospective customers, thus accelerating the sales cycle.

Retention and Referrals

Customer *retention* results from delighted customers. Happy customers provide up-sell and cross-sell opportunities—plus strong *referrals*.

Rewards and Recognition

Alignment of all members of the sales team, from senior management to director to manager to salesperson, is vital to ensure that everyone is pulling in the same direction. Rewarding productive behaviors at all levels helps accomplish this.

Enablement

Enablement leads the "E" portion of the MORE Sales Framework. Training your salespeople to understand your offerings is critical. They need a thorough understanding of your messaging, your solution, and how your solution solves problems, how it delivers outcomes, and what makes you different from the competition.

Essential Sales Tools

One-time training events are easily forgotten. *Essential sales tools* provide repetition that will solidify your salespeople's knowledge and skills, allowing them to deliver your message confidently and completely. Consistent messages must also permeate your website, digital marketing, mobile messaging, and social media. In addition, there is an abundance of software selling tools and plugins to help make sales more efficient, consistent, and predictable.

Execution

Finally, the most important (though often overlooked) element for achieving MORE sales is execution.

Execution means carrying out the plan, optimizing the processes, reaching the objectives, implementing the metrics, and constantly ensuring that your company creates delightful outcomes. A brilliant plan that isn't executed isn't worth the paper it's printed on.

From here, the 12 MORE sales elements are broken into short chapters with real-world examples. Small start-up companies and large multinational corporations have implemented these principles with extraordinary success. We know you can, too. Here's to driving MORE sales!

Patricia Watkins
& Dan Doster

ONE

Market

Identifying the right audience for a particular offering seems easy enough, doesn't it? But did you know that one of the top reasons new offerings fail is because the right market goes unidentified?

Too many companies don't ask the right questions: *Where is our market?*, or, more to the point, *Who feels the pain that our offering solves?* The stakes are high. Misidentify your audience, and your superior offering may not stand much of a chance.

© marketoonist.com

So, assuming you already have a product that works, let's focus on identifying your target market, first defining it, and then refining it.

Define and Understand Your Market

"… the first thing you want to do is understand the market. You want to go out there and map the competitive landscape. You want to know what your customers are saying."

BRIAN FRANK,
GLOBAL HEAD OF SALES OPERATIONS AT LINKEDIN

Let's start here: What are some relevant market trends? Who is the economic buyer with true budget control over any purchase? These and other answers can be discerned through the clutter with a little research in several areas:

- Market research
- Competitive analyses
- Economic modeling
- Prospect profiling

In the technology market, sources of market research and competitive analysis can include Gartner, Forrester, Nielsen, Kantar, comScore, or other industry experts. Start with their assessments of projected market growth, market leaders, and critical competitors. Who is on the rise, and why? What is your unique advantage or differentiation? Are you competitive on price and benefits? Will a winning price deliver profits?

Economic modeling is essential to understanding your subsector's business models, margins, pricing structures, and strategies. The variables you need to consider include: what are the projected expenses and income based on your different strategies? What's the overall cost of sales in pursuing your market? How much of a profit will your target markets realize? How much investment is needed? What ROI will it bring? Different financial models might be required for alternate scenarios.

Use each selected target market to profile your top prospects. What is the specific role (or title) of the ideal buyer? Is it the chief information officer? The chief marketing officer? The chief information security officer? The vice president of operations? The line of business owner? If you approach at too high or too low a level, you could find yourself in a sales cycle that's either quickly dashed or unnecessarily prolonged.

© 2011 Ted Goff www.tedgoff.com

**"I'd like to speak to your CEO or
CIO or COO or receptionist.
It doesn't matter which."**

Here's an important question: do you even have access to the target market? Does your product offering meet a need in Europe, the Middle East, Africa, or Asia? Do you meet the regulatory and legal requirements of those regions? Can you acquire the necessary business licenses and infrastructure? Are you aware of the local customs, and even taboos? What about the language? The word "football," for instance, means something different in the United States than what it means almost everywhere else in the world. How will your offering translate in a foreign country? Examples abound of failed marketing messages that were lost on the target audience or even ended up offending its recipients. Being thorough in assessing these matters is critical.

Early questions on potential market viability include knowing whether the market is large enough to be profitable, whether it can grow fast enough to be sustainable, and whether it has a wide enough moat to discourage potential competitors.

Depending on these initial market conditions, you can make an early go/no-go decision. Or, revisit and refine your definition of your target market perhaps a little, perhaps a lot. Or, you may simply seek additional market research. You should not proceed unless you can successfully pass through these gates.

Refine your Market Plan

Market research will help identify the Total Addressable Market (TAM) for your offerings, both quantitatively and qualitatively. Is it a growing market or a declining one? Is the TAM large and robust enough for success? If so, where in that larger market is the greatest opportunity for success? Refine your market segmentation by geography, industry, and specific prospects.

Given the problems you solve and the outcomes you deliver, what vertical markets have the most pain your solution can alleviate? Does your solution fit especially well in specific verticals such as financial, insurance, retail, energy, healthcare, transportation, entertainment, telecommunications, technology services, or some other vertical?

You'll also need to consider how to address geographic coverage. You'll want a go-to-market plan that anticipates defined territories with a clear idea as to how those territories will be covered.

Sales Execution

Once the market plan is finalized, it's time to carefully examine the prerequisite for excellent sales execution: How will you cover those prospective accounts and/or territory with the necessary sales and support resources? Will you use marketing development representatives (MDRs), sales development representatives (SDRs), inside sales reps, field sales reps, or reseller and channel partners? (We'll cover these different sales resources in more detail in upcoming chapters.) Will you offer online sales? How much and what type of sales support will be required and will this vary by target market and geography? Answers to these questions will help you further prioritize and refine your target market definitions.

But first, validate the target market (or markets) you've selected with a well-tested approach for pursuing each market. Pair your offerings with each target market. Then, develop a phased approach with timelines and goals to improve your chances of success. An effective test is to pick a few good pilot customers. These can provide invaluable feedback highlighting needed adjustments to your go-to-market offering. They'll also serve as early proof points and references.

> *"No business can be all things to all people.*
> *Instead, you must reach specific customers and satisfy their*
> *particular needs ... you must identify those customers*
> *and understand as precisely as possible what they want."*

ALLBUSINESS NETWORKS

Once there's proven success with pilot accounts, pick a few prospects as "lighthouse" accounts—sector leaders who can give you credibility within your target market. Put a full-court press on working with these prospects to solve their business problems with your solution. Make sure you provide an exceptional experience. Then feature them as references in your early marketing efforts, before a full roll-out is underway. But take good care of them. Companies know that they're lighthouse accounts and can publicly withdraw support if not treated with considerable care and respect.

Understand Your Prospects and Ideal Customer Profiles

It's one thing to have a list of prospective accounts. It's another matter entirely to *understand* your accounts and know why they would be good prospects for your offerings. It's essential to know who your ideal customer is within your defined market and what problems most concern them.

Not long ago, the research company Forrester found that just 22 percent of customers believe their sales reps "understand [their] issues."[1] Let's put that another way: *78 percent* of customers *don't* believe their sales reps understand their problems. Make sure your teams don't fall victim to this unacceptable scenario. Sales reps exist to solve business problems and deliver positive outcomes. How can you prescribe a solution if you don't understand the problems that your prospective decision-makers are facing?

> *"Nearly 57% of B2B prospects and customers feel that their sales teams are not prepared for the first meeting."*

IDC

Some sales reps just "show up and throw up." You know these guys. They simply just start talking, asking few questions, too eager to tell you everything, whether it's applicable or not, and showing you every slide in their decks. First things first: do your research and listen to your prospect's needs. And avoid focusing on slide decks as your only means of communicating!

Today, researching prospects is all too easy and there are no excuses for not doing so. You can start with a Google search. Also, look at the prospect's 10K and read the chairman or CEO's Letter

---

[1] Q4 2013 North America and Europe Executive Buyer Insight Survey by Forrester Research, Inc.

to the Shareholders to understand the prospect's direction and top initiatives. You can read about the people you're going to meet on LinkedIn. Tools like RainKing, Hoovers, and others provide a wealth of timely information on companies. Learn about the prospect's industry and related trends. See the lists below for some examples of available resources.

Free Resources for Prospect Research:

- Company website

- Chairman's Letter to the Shareholders

- SEC documents (annual reports, 10Ks, proxy statements)

- Statement (DEF 14A) for executive compensation and to understand which financial metrics are important

- Analyst reports (both free and fee)

- Investor relations website

- Press releases

- LinkedIn profiles

- Top competitors

- Industry publications

Fee-Based Resources for Prospect Research:

- RainKing, DiscoverOrg, InsideView, Owler, iProfile, Hoovers, BoardEx (sales intelligence databases)

- Salesforce Data.com, Zoominfo, Salesgenie, YesData (prospecting databases)

- MarketVision (market research, competition & trends)

- First Research (industry profiles, industry intelligence tools)
- ProQuest (library news database)

There are countless sources of information available today. Check the web or check with others in your company or network to find additional resources best suited to your target market and offerings.

Above all else, understanding your prospect's needs comes down to *listening*. Before even thinking about prescribing anything, be sure you understand what the problems are. And qualify them based on the relevancy of your solution. Don't force-fit. Do both parties a favor and walk away if your solution won't solve the prospect's pain.

"How can I learn about your company's needs if you keep interrupting me?"

"Most people think "selling" is the same as "talking". But the most effective salespeople know that listening is the most important part of their job."

ROY BARTELL

If you do your homework, keeping in mind Forrester's twenty-two-percent statistic, your sales team will be miles ahead of the great majority of the competition's salespeople.

In Our Experience

For start-up projects (both large and small) with limited resources, we've found it vital to create well-researched go-to-market business plans, thus ensuring deployment of the company's resources where there was the greatest probability of success. For us, the key to getting additional funding (both internally and externally) has been to make certain the investments enhanced our ability to *deliver on expectations*. For some companies, we've needed to adjust the direction several times to get the model properly focused. We learned by listening to pilot and lighthouse customers, and by keeping our fingers on the pulse of the industry, the competition, and the trends. And we adjusted as conditions dictated.

In defining sales coverage, our teams would put together a target list of suspects and map them geographically. We wanted to understand the markets, the problems the offerings could solve, and how the prospects and customers were geographically dispersed. Defining the market and the target territories were key factors in determining what sales resources were needed domestically and internationally. And, we needed to understand where to put the resources to ensure that everyone had a patch in which they could be successful.

Of course, there are times when you need to change direction. On one team, although we knew the market, the ideal customer profile changed. At that company, there was an exceptional history of successfully selling to chief information officers (CIOs). But with chief marketing officers (CMOs) becoming more critical in the decision-making process for the new solutions we were offering, we needed to enable our sales teams to become better prepared for pursuing conversations with CMOs. We needed to research the needs of the CMOs, their desired outcomes, their industries, and the specific needs of their companies. We held internal webinars on a global basis to help our sales teams become more comfortable with the tools available to better understand their markets and customers. We trained them on how to approach a CMO versus a CIO, and which different problems they typically needed to solve.

You can do a great job of defining your target market; however, to drive more sales, focusing on the ideal customer profile and *effective sales execution* are essential.

Summary

Remember, to optimize your market definition

- Research your market,
- Understand your competition and what makes your offering unique,
- Build an economic model,
- Define your ideal customer profile,
- Conduct pilots and select lighthouse accounts,
- Be prepared to adjust when necessary.

Market definition and validation are essential. Going too broad too early can dilute your efforts. Rather, define a target market where you have a competitive advantage.

Defining and refining your *market* is your first step. Then, you need to define and refine your *messaging*. Let's cover that next.

TWO

Messaging

"Great content is the best sales tool in the world."

Marcus Sheridan

Branding encompasses the overall image of a company's offerings, including logo, tagline, even a commercial jingle. It's built over time, influenced by the company's own advertising as well as by customer experience and perception. Think of branding as the long-term culmination of impressions. Think of messaging, addressed here, as more tactical and more specific. Messaging affirms or reinforces the brand and includes advertising, websites, social media, sales pitches, and word of mouth.

"85% of companies agree their sales team's ability to articulate value messages is the single most critical factor in closing deals."

CORPORATE VISIONS

No organization is immune from poor messaging and message misalignment. A few years ago, we led a demand-generation, business-process re-engineering project for the executive staff of a Fortune 500 company. There were over 100 different countries within the scope of the company, each developing its own messaging. Minor variations with local languages were expected and understandable.

But the overall problem went far beyond minor translation issues. There simply was no single *core* message that everyone could rally around. Instead, millions of dollars had been spent in a duplication of marketing efforts.

© 2002 Ted Goff

"Snowballs? I thought we were discussing coconuts."

In this case, our approach was to identify sales and marketing associates from across the globe, with proven track records, to assist us on a full-time basis with this six-month project. In the discovery phase, we exposed a serious disconnect between sales reps and marketing personnel. Sales rejected marketing's messaging. Marketing dismissed the sales organization as simply ineffective. That's not uncommon. But here, marketing itself was internally misaligned as well. Each country had its own independent marketing organization; each with messaging different from its peers—a highly ineffective and high-cost approach.

Let's cover some of the basics of messaging and then walk through the steps we took to help this company.

Change WIIFM to WIIFT

An effective message about your offering starts by remembering that it's centered on the *prospect* and the problems the prospect is trying to solve. It's not about you, your company, or even your solution. What's In It For Me (WIIFM) must become What's In It For Them. Why is your solution of value *to them*? What problem are *they* experiencing? How can you help them achieve the outcome they want? Specifically:

- Can you resolve a global problem of theirs?

- Can you reduce their costs?

- Can you reduce their time to market?

- Can you renew their focus on innovation?

- Can you increase their revenues?

- Can you increase their productivity?

- Can you improve their customer satisfaction?

- Can you reduce their risk?

- Can you increase their compliance?

- Can you increase their security?

- What are their top strategic initiatives, and how does your solution address one or more of them?

Notice the word "their" in each of the above items. We all know intuitively that solutions for our customers are of no value unless they solve *their* problems. But all too often, this gets forgotten.

Develop Your Elevator Pitch

Once you understand WIIFT—their desired outcome—begin developing an "elevator pitch," so named because such a message ought to be concise enough for a sales rep to communicate it to a prospect during a short elevator ride. Figure about thirty seconds to grab the prospect's attention before reaching his or her floor. Developing a carefully refined pitch takes time and multiple iterations, but in the end, you'll have a concise and non-conflicted message that can be delivered in person (or by voicemail, email, social media, and other digital options). Make sure to include these critical components:

- We offer X,

- Which solves Y problem.

- We're uniquely differentiated from our competitors because of Z.

- We've solved problems with marquee customers in your industry including A, B, and C.

A rule of thumb is to simplify your pitch to between 25 and 75 words (assuming most people can effectively communicate, or hear, 150 words a minute).

After you've defined your message, test it, validate it, and refine it. Seek alignment—ensure your sales reps and all others who interact with customers have easy access to, and a clear understanding of, the elevator pitch. Make certain your messaging is tightly aligned between sales and marketing personnel and programs. Your messaging needs to be consistent throughout your organization and everyone needs to be on the same page. Alignment is an essential and best practice.

> *"Companies with tightly aligned sales and marketing teams achieved an average 32% annual revenue growth, far better than less aligned companies."*
>
> THE ABERDEEN GROUP

Moving forward from your elevator pitch, you can begin to wrap more compelling information around it. Include the exact words of your elevator pitch (or at least a subset of them) in brochures, in slide presentations, and, very importantly, in social media.

In fact, social media can be used by all of your employees to share your message with your prospective customers. This is *employee advocacy* at work—creating content that your employees will be excited about and proud to share with their social media network. It further enhances their brand as a trusted advisor and will often be better received than the company's direct social media messaging.

Remember, there is value to both your employees and your prospects in hearing the same consistent, compelling messages, and in being able to easily reiterate them.

Sing Your Accolades

When it comes to messaging, don't forget to tout your accolades. If, for example, you can say you're in Gartner's Leader's Quadrant, that would signify important market validation to your prospects. Promote all your industry accolades—Gartner, Forrester, Forbes, Great Places to Work, local recognition, technology awards, etc. These kinds of recommendations and endorsements are especially important in today's social media environment.

Call to Action

Effective messaging is above all else a call to action—a meeting, a discovery session, a workshop, a demo, a thirty-day trial, a download of a white paper, or a special time-stamped promotion.

The Many Ways Your Prospects Learn About You

According to a recent survey, *57 percent* of the typical business-to-business (B2B) customer's decision-making process is done *before* he or she even contacts a potential supplier. Some respondents reported being as much as 70 percent complete in their decision making before reaching out to potential suppliers.[2]

It's no surprise that digital, social, and mobile marketing are crucial platforms for effective marketing. Digital media include technology-based platforms such as websites, blogs, online magazines, cloud-based applications, and other web-based avenues. Social media include Facebook, Twitter, LinkedIn, Instagram, Snapchat, Pinterest, YouTube, Vimeo, and other platforms that are available to communicate your sales messaging. As for mobile marketing, Google reports a 91-percent growth in the use of mobile applications since 2012 throughout the entire purchasing path (rather than at just the initial stages of research). And not only are prospects using mobile applications to search, read, and compare products and

---

[2] Survey by the global best practice insights and technology company CEB, now Gartner.

brands, they're using mobile to make their purchases, too. Even in the B2B world. (You might want to ask your prospects just where and how they're getting *their* information!)

> *"89% of B2B researchers use the Internet during the research process. But looking closer at this group reveals an even more important trend: almost half (46%) are 18–34-year-olds. These are the millenials."*

> *"If you're not marketing to this group, you need to reevaluate your strategy, taking into account millennials' familiarity with digital and how this influences the kind of content and media channels they are using."*

"The Changing Face of B2B Marketing,"
Kelsey Snyder & Pashmeena Hilal from *Think With Google*.

But even in today's digital world, there's still old-fashioned word-of-mouth marketing. As opposed to more traditional forms of marketing, 84 percent of people, according to research from Nielsen, trust recommendations from friends and family. That same Nielsen study revealed that the second most trusted advertising source is content-based advertising.

Content marketing is a means of keeping in touch with your customers and potential customers by delivering them useful information rather than a sales pitch. Effective content marketing means that when your prospects are ready to buy, they'll look to you—an unmistakable expert or thought leader in your field.

"Content marketing is a strategic marketing approach focused on creating and distributing valuable, relevant, and consistent content to attract and retain a clearly-defined audience — and, ultimately, to drive profitable customer action."

CONTENT MARKETING INSTITUTE

Examples of content marketing:

- "How-to" content

- Guides

- Learning Center videos

- Free valuable ideas and advice

- Blogs

Finally, your message can also be effectively delivered by your salespeople—with the help of whiteboards, slide decks, e-mail, a LinkedIn Inmail, or even a voicemail. This is when a consistent elevator pitch can be most important.

Also, keep in mind that relationships can be crucial in sales, and a little personal touch can go a long way towards encouraging customers to buy from you.

Consistency and Uniqueness

Beyond asking if your message is consistent, is it also unique to your company and product offering? Can it be differentiated from your competitors' messages? With a Fortune 500 client, we had a simple test for gauging uniqueness: could our client's company name be swapped out with the name of any competitor? Could that competitor say or claim the exact same things?

What, in other words, makes your organization's product or service different?

In Our Experience

Let's return to the above case of the Fortune 500 company with messaging that was inconsistent globally. We spoke to sales and marketing groups around the world. Focus groups were held. Surveys were conducted. Best practices, both inside and outside the company, were researched. One critical conclusion was to establish a core team from around the globe to evaluate the best messaging and practices for creating and rolling out communications.

The objectives were achieved and at a significantly reduced cost. In fact, the plan's objectives were exceeded, saving tens of millions of dollars in the first year, reducing overall SG&A, and providing superior demand-generation deliverables.

How did we achieve these results? We recognized that a separate, fully-staffed marketing group in each country was unnecessary. Each country was an extension of a larger entity and they all worked in collaboration, leveraging the resources and best practices of the global team. Instead of everyone recreating the wheel, we pooled our collective best thinking. Each message and every deliverable was battle-tested, validated, and reviewed by trusted sales and marketing resources in each region. It was no longer *us* versus *them*. It became *we*. Only with global alignment, did we market our deliverables. The deliverables (messaging that went into tools, training, manuals, and other information media) were met with open arms and turned into outstanding results.

With collaboration, you'll end up with better reception and higher adoption internally, and a broader feeling of ownership across both sales and marketing.

Summary

How to optimize the messaging element of the MORE Sales Framework:

- Remember WIIFT.

- Define and refine your elevator pitch.

- Broadcast accolades.

- Create a call to action.

- Leverage digital, social, mobile, and content marketing.

- Align sales and marketing.

Messaging is vitally important to driving MORE sales. It's imperative to have a clear, crisp, differentiated message that resonates with the audience and solves a customer's problem, achieves a goal, delivers outcomes, or eliminates or reduces an unnecessary hurdle. Achieving customers' outcomes is such an important aspect of effective selling that we've dedicated a subsequent chapter to it. And, in the chapter on essential sales tools, we'll discuss how to leverage your messaging, increase its adoption, and drive it consistently.

Now you've defined your *market* and your *messaging*. The next key step is to define your *metrics*. How will you track and measure sales?

THREE

Metrics

"What gets measured gets done."

LORD KELVIN

To a large extent, the practice of sales is a numbers-based game. More prospects and more proposals mean more potential wins. But what's the result? More attempts? Or more losses? Bottom line: know the effectiveness of your sales activity. Years ago, there was an adage: for every ten "no's," you'll get one "yes." That meant that a salesperson could enjoy getting a "no" because each one was getting him or her just that much closer to a "yes." It was, and still is, a numbers game. As such, there are many metrics to consider using.

Here's another rule-of-thumb that's been around a while: two percent of direct marketing efforts result in leads. If true in your situation, then sending more direct marketing pieces or emails *will* eventually yield an outcome. Advertising, both print and digital, trade shows, webinars, and social media are examples of additional ways to create leads. The questions are these: is your current lead generation the most efficient way to create awareness and—the real key—*preference* for your offering? Are there other mediums that can be used to garner more awareness, possibly at a reduced cost? How many leads are you creating? What is your lead conversion rate, for example? Are your leads high quality leads? How many leads are turning into qualified opportunities?

How critical is it to know the answers to these questions? Remember the statistic from the previous chapter? Fifty-seven percent of the typical B2B customer's decision-making process is done before he or she even contacts a potential supplier. That means you need to have metrics by which to measure how successful your messaging is prior to a salesperson getting involved.

Some metrics are easier to ascertain than others. The quality of leads from digital and social media, for instance, can be difficult to track, but critical nonetheless. Ultimately, no matter your avenues of marketing and promotion, you need to know how many leads turn into qualified prospects.

Just as metrics gleaned from your marketing efforts are the key to driving more sales leads, metrics gleaned from your sales efforts are the key to driving more sales. Without accurate measurements, without a tracking mechanism, there's no way to monitor both what's working and what's not working, and, consequently, what specifically to modify.

While selling is both art and science, in this chapter we'll focus on the science. Coaching a salesperson on sales effectiveness and technique would require a book of a different type, and plenty are out there. For our purposes, we want to consider the numbers. Sales inputs and outputs can be measured. Further, the results can be seen by both management and sales reps alike in regular reports or dashboards. Think of the dashboard in your car. It contains the key information or vital signs to drive your car. In sales, a dashboard provides the key information or vital signs you need to drive more sales. The great news is that if you manage the numbers, you have a higher probability of positively impacting the results, and sooner rather than later. If you don't measure, you often won't know what you're lacking until it's too late.

Basic Sales Metrics

There are many metrics that can be applied to measure sales activity, including the lofty list below:

Business & Operating Metrics	• Revenue, Gross Margins, Cost of Sale, Targets, YoY Growth • Product/Service Adoption, Geography • Direct vs Influenced vs Partner Influenced Revenue
Customer Metrics	• MRR – New (Land), Expansion (Expand), Churn (Retain), MoM Growth • Services Attach Rates, Deferred Bookings/Revenue, NPS, Adoption, Usage • Retention, Lifetime Value (LTV), Customer Acquisition Cost (CAC)
Direct Sales & Partner Metrics	• Sales (WTD, MTD, QTD, YTD), Growth %, Product/Solutions Sold, Targets • Forecasting, Opportunity Pipeline, Conversion Ratios, Average Deal Size, Cycle Time, Strategic Value & Impact, New and Expansion Pipeline • Marketing Metrics – Lead Volume/Source, Cost per Lead, MQLs, SQLs
Sales Performance Metrics	• Performance by Sales Rep to Target (MTD, QTD, YTD) • Opportunity Pipeline by Rep, by Product/Solution, by Geography, Average Selling Price, Sales Cycle Times, Ramp Time • Conversion Ratios, Value Selling and Qualification Criteria

"Thompson, I need you to redefine key metrics through dynamic optimization alignment. The rest of you, figure out what that means."

In this chapter, we'll focus on three of the most fundamental metrics your sales teams must embrace:

1   Sales opportunity pipeline or funnel

2   Close rates

3   Average selling price

Other metrics can be developed to peel back the onion if these metrics don't provide the depth of information needed. That said, a common mistake is to develop too many metrics, which can create a lack of focus on these three important ones. Remember that, in the end, the objective is to achieve your sales goals.

Sales Opportunity Pipeline

The *sales opportunity pipeline* includes all sales opportunities from the initial stage of lead identification to the final close, with estimated close dates in the given sales periods.

Things to consider in assessing your pipeline:

- What percent of the overall pipeline is in each sales phase?

- How many days are spent in each phase of the pipeline? (Only observing the average can be deceiving.)

- What is limiting your ability to accelerate into the next stage of the pipeline?

- How qualified are the opportunities in the pipeline? (You'll find more about qualification in Chapter 5 on Optimized Sales Processes.)

- What's the length of your typical sales cycle? Can you shorten the sales cycle to reduce cycle time? (Again, see Chapter 5 on Optimized Sales Processes.)

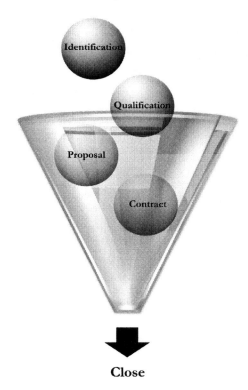

Close

The other aspect of tracking your pipeline is to ensure you have enough in your pipeline to meet your objectives. And you need to ensure that there are always new leads coming in to keep the pipeline full. Tracking all the moving parts is crucial to sales success.

Close Rates

Close rate is the ratio of the total number of qualified leads converted to closed sales. You simply take the number of closed sales and divide it by the number of all qualified leads. For example, if you have 20 qualified leads, and you close 5, you have a close ratio of 5/20, or a 25-percent *close rate*. Simple math.

Close rates can vary significantly based on complexity, market conditions, price points, competitive offerings, etc. In the tech industry, we have seen close rates between 20 and 50 percent, but, of course, this will fluctuate by sub-industry and can be affected by the pricing strategy. Some companies, especially if they have a lot of incoming unqualified leads, use a close rate based on all opportunities and leads, and a separate close rate based just on "qualified" opportunities and leads. Other companies focus on "win" rates that can be calculated by dividing the dollar value of the revenue by the dollar value of qualified leads. There's no single best method.

A significantly low close rate might reflect a pipeline that is perhaps very large and unqualified. Maybe there's a potential need to further qualify the leads, with the marketing department, for example, taking more of a qualifying role before the leads reach the salespeople. A significantly low close rate might also reflect a lack of closing skills. Or maybe it's a combination of insufficient qualification plus unsatisfactory selling skills. One thing is sure: you'll never know if you don't track your close rates.

Average Selling Price

Average Selling Price (ASP), also known as average deal size or average transaction size, is an important indicator of sales effectiveness with respect to measuring the value of your product or service in the mind of the customer versus the value offered by the competition.

Observing the changes in average selling price, after several quarters of selling a new offering or product, as well as noting the variability between sales reps and between sales territories, can be highly instructive when it comes to coaching and training sales reps in promoting a value-based approach with their prospects and customers.

In addition to improving the effectiveness of value-based selling, it's possible to increase the average selling price by up-selling or selling add-ons and new features. We'll further discuss pricing and the pricing process in Chapter 5 on Optimized Sales Processes.

Below is an example of the pipeline needed, based on the quota (for example, a sales target assigned to a sales rep), the ASP, and the close rate.

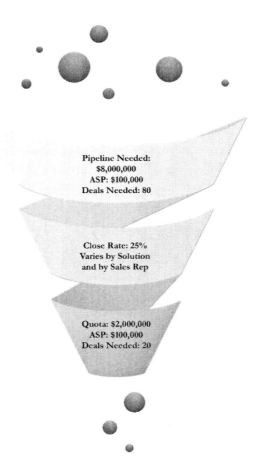

Pipeline Needed:
$8,000,000
ASP: $100,000
Deals Needed: 80

Close Rate: 25%
Varies by Solution
and by Sales Rep

Quota: $2,000,000
ASP: $100,000
Deals Needed: 20

1 In this example, the annual quota is $2,000,000, the ASP is $100,000. As such, the rep needs to close 20 deals.

2 Assume the close rate for that rep is 25%.

3 Based on that, $8,000,000 is needed in the pipeline. With an ASP of $100,000, 80 deals are needed in the pipeline.

And if for example, your close rate or ASP goes down, you'll need more deals in the pipeline. To achieve your goals, you must keep your eyes on the numbers.

Other Potential Metrics

As noted earlier, there's no shortage of metrics that your company may want or need to track.

Monthly Recurring Revenue (MRR) for subscription-based offerings such as Cloud and SaaS solutions is an important metric to understand. Be sure your revenue is going up each month, not down. It's important to track the MRR for churn and to track your incremental sales, making sure your incremental sales exceed your churn. A 10-percent increase in new sales, for instance, with a 20-percent churn rate means you're going backwards. (Churn can be managed by delighting your customers. We'll talk about how to do just that in Chapter 8 on Retention and Referrals.)

Here are some additional metrics you might decide to use:

- Track sales *by timeframe*. Know your sales by month, quarter, year, so you can track trends over time and anticipate seasonality.

- Track your conversion rates *within each sales stage* to determine effectiveness and to see what's bogging down the process.

- Track sales *by products and services*. What are your hot sellers? What's not selling? With this information, you can put plans in place to market some items more aggressively or investigate why other items aren't selling.

- Track *lead sources*. Inbound, marketing development representatives, sales development representatives, advertising, referral, promotion, etc. Where are your leads coming from? Tracking these trends can help you increase those sources that are providing the greatest success, and reduce or eliminate those that are proving less impactful.

- Track whether your purchasers are *new customers or existing customers*.

- Track *percentage through each channel.* Know what portion of your sales are sold directly through field sales, inside sales, and through channel partners.

Pay attention as well to your *sales cycle timeline* (we'll review this in more detail in Chapter 5 on Optimized Sales Processes). If you can compress your sales cycles, you can also expand your effectiveness. For example, if you can reduce the time it takes to close, you can drive up your sales velocity.

Beware! It *is* possible to create too many metrics. Yes, managing by metrics is important, but you can over-inspect. Metrics should be actionable and/or insightful. If they aren't, then they're simply not useful. An over-use of metrics could result in bogged down sales productivity. Worse, you might even discover you're driving down morale.

It's certainly not easy to significantly improve any given metric. But there are a few metrics that, if improved, can significantly impact your results. If, for example, managing lots of deals in a year is unrealistic, then you might be wise to consider driving up your ASP and close rates. But understanding your metrics comes before pursuing any strategy changes.

Align Sales and Marketing

In the last chapter, we discussed how results can be significantly improved when sales and marketing are aligned. When it comes to metrics, and yielding better results, this alignment is critical. Studies have shown that well-aligned sales and marketing teams can account for a 15 percent increase in win rate. And according to a study by Altify, high performers are 57 percent more likely to come from companies where sales and marketing are well-aligned.

Marketing plays a key role in creating awareness, which has a significant impact on pipeline growth. As we've discussed, the better qualified the leads, the higher the close rates. That translates into a more efficient sales cycle and better use of your salespeople's time. Further, marketing can assist with packaging or bundling, and promotions for up-sell and cross-sell opportunities to drive up the ASP. When sales and marketing are working in lockstep, the results can be profoundly improved.

In Our Experience

In our experience, the three metrics that are critical to every sales organization are the size of pipeline, the close ratio, and the average selling price. Staying focused on these metrics helps achieve your objectives.

On one of our high-performance "tiger" sales teams, we crafted a strategy in support of our objectives and then tracked the corresponding metrics with the goal of doubling our sales each year. Now, that may not be what we said to "the Street," but tiger teams are most effective when they're ambitious.

*"Shoot for the moon, and even if you miss,
you'll be among the stars."*

LES BROWN

If our goal was to grow by 20 percent, we'd shoot for 40 percent. We focused on driving more opportunities by driving more engagements (our pipeline), increasing our solution offerings (our ASP), and raising our close rates (through training and better hiring practices).

To drive up our ASP, we looked at bundles—solutions that effectively were more compelling as a group than if sold separately. Or, we bundled solutions that were complementary so that combining them drove the price lower than if the solutions were purchased separately, yet drove the ASP higher. Then we focused on increasing our close rate. For example, if we only closed 10 percent of our deals, we had to have a pipeline 10 times our objective. If we closed 25 percent of our deals, we needed a pipeline of 4 times. And so we focused on better qualifying our pipeline, moving poorly qualified deals out of the pipeline and sending them back to MDRs, SDRs, or the marketing department for them to continue their nurture campaigns. We looked at what we had in each stage of the pipeline (what realistically could be closed) and what needed to be done to accelerate the process (average time in each stage).

Better qualified leads led to better close ratios. We developed "close plans" (which we'll cover in more detail in Chapter 12) and we had weekly reviews for all of our top deals in the quarter. We considered such factors as the competition, critical dates, key contacts, as well as other areas that would help us map out our strategy. We met weekly as a team to discuss the close plans, to learn from each other, to explore where we had seen similar situations, and to discover where we could help each other address challenges or leverage our successes. Everyone on the team benefited from the discussions. Collectively, we increased our close rate, significantly increased our forecast predictability, and ultimately delivered better than expected results.

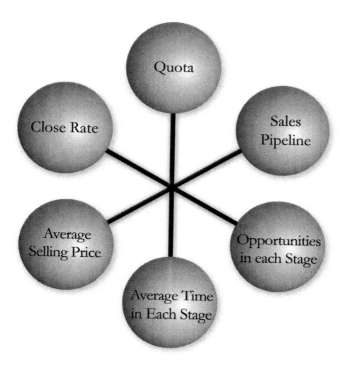

Summary

To improve the metrics to drive MORE sales:

- Focus on the sales opportunity pipeline.

- Increase close rates.

- Expand average selling price.

- Align sales and marketing.

An entire book could be written on all of the potential metrics you could use to measure and manage your sales results. In this chapter, we focused on the key metrics: pipeline, close rate, and average selling price. Whatever you use, your metrics are critical in managing your business proactively. By getting ahead of the numbers and managing them, you'll increase your productivity and predictability.

What gets measured gets done.

Without these measurements, there's no tracking mechanism by which to monitor both what's working, and what's not working.

In the next section, we'll discuss the "O" elements of the MORE Sales Framework: Operations, Optimized Sales Processes, and Outcomes. It's great to set goals, but the key is to measure and manage them efficiently. Operations can have a significant impact on managing your results, increasing sales productivity as well as improving the important goal of customer delight.

FOUR

Operations

*"Today, 30 to 35 percent of a salesperson's face time
is spent with the customer. Salespeople spend too much
time on administrating, expediting orders, arguing over
receivables, and finding late shipments."*

JACK WELCH,
FORMER CEO, GENERAL ELECTRIC

A re your sales reps spending most their time in front of customers, or doing administrative work? To improve your sales results, you need to remove as much of the administrative burden from the sales organization as possible. The goal is for sales to be focused on selling. Managing the internal and back office duties is the job of *operations*.

The operations function is typically located organizationally in the finance, administration, or sales operations department. No matter where it's located, its function in helping sales must include more than merely delivering reports and dashboards, important as they may be. Operations must ensure that credit checks are completed. It needs to confirm that revenue recognition guidelines are followed, that contracts are adhered to, and that orders are written and processed properly. The functions of operations should also include tracking shipments and verifying that the customers receive what they've ordered, on time. Operations must make certain that customers' outcomes are achieved. Operations needs to ensure exceptional customer experiences and, in short, customer delight.

The primary deliverables of operations might include the following, each of which we'll address in greater detail below:

- Forecasting of sales metrics

- Dashboards

- Pricing support and bid desk

- Contracting

- Revenue recognition

For our purposes, operations refers to all non-selling functions that consume sales time. The activities can therefore be wide-ranging, and might further include some or many of the following: onboarding, automation of the sales processes, evaluation of sales methodologies, training, sales strategy, the go-to-market model, territory management, lead distribution, data management, CRM support, compensation, and general administration.

The leaders of the various operations' functions are critical partners of the head of sales and everyone in the sales organization. Because, for example, financial accounting rules govern the company's transactions, the finance lead is a key partner of the sales leader.

Everything regarding sales operations is inextricably linked with sales, regardless of where any operation's function reports.

"71% of sales reps say they spend too much time on data entry."

TOUTAPP

©Glasbergen
glasbergen.com

"Before we begin our Time Management Seminar, did everyone get one of these 36-hour wrist watches?"

Forecasting Reviews

Managing your individual and team numbers is important for monitoring and achieving more sales. It's one thing for operations to track all of your numbers; it's another to ensure everyone in sales has *ownership* of the numbers.

In one company we were involved with, operations sent forecasts every Sunday to sales leadership (the sales directors and VPs). On Mondays, the head of operations held a conference call at 8:00 a.m. with the VPs and the executive staff reviewing and committing to our numbers for the next week, month, and quarter. We often discussed the largest deals in the pipeline as well. Of course, with today's technology, most forecast data can be accessed directly from sales reporting tools but the key point is that the data need to be reviewed and discussed. All involved need to feel ownership and commit to achieving the expected results.

Following our Monday meetings, the sales VPs and their operations liaison would meet with our sales directors to review their forecasts. If they were behind in meeting our overall objectives, we would discuss what each team needed to do to fill the gap to the plan or to resolve the risk to the forecast.

The focus was always on how to help everyone meet their goals and overcome any obstacles to meet their overall objectives. It was important that the reviews not be onerous or painful, but rather for them to collectively provide a process that yielded benefits to the sales organization, always answering the question: *How can the sales teams be assisted in meeting their goals?*

Following those calls were one-on-one meetings throughout the week with sales directors and their individual reports to review their forecast numbers and determine where they could use assistance. On this level, too, the key was not to create an uncomfortable performance inspection, but to make sure that everyone was working together to ensure that all were tracking to plan, and, if they were not, to put immediate corrective action in place to assist the sales rep. The objective was to be proactive so that no gaps were discovered too late in the month or quarter to make a correction. At the end of the week, all of the teams rolled up their numbers to operations. Operations would consolidate them and provide the overall metrics that would then be presented in the executive staff call the following Monday morning.

Naturally, the specific method for conducting forecast reviews is less important than that they occur on regular intervals.

Dashboards and Reports

Reports and dashboards are critical tools for not only upper management but also sales reps and their immediate sales management. Seeing a visual representation of the rep's forecast and sales results on a daily basis can be especially effective. The key is for the sales reps to feel ownership of the data as well as accountability for it.

Dashboards can be created and then released at the beginning of each week, perhaps each Sunday, for example, to each sales rep's inbox as well as his or her respective management's inbox. This allows the sales organization to proactively drive closure on the sales reps' forecasted opportunities and to address any opportunities that need additional attention.

Dashboards are an effective way for sales reps to see how they are doing with respect to their objectives; for VPs, directors, and managers to see how their teams are performing against other peer groups; and, importantly, to give the sales organization a broad, yet detailed view of the entire business.

Pricing

Pricing controls and discount guidelines are typically established within a company to ensure that financial results (sales and profits) are maximized. That said, parameters are typically set by general management, including the CEO, COO, and marketing, while considering other outside variables such as government regulations, legal requirements, and competitor alternatives. Pricing is a governing factor, therefore, of strategy.

But this can present some difficulties. For example, pricing may report to the chief financial officer (CFO) or the head of marketing or the head of sales. Depending upon the nature of the offer, the company, the clients, or competitive landscape, there may be more (or less) discipline in the process to ensure that pricing parameters are maintained. This structure, however, can sometimes create unhealthy antagonism between the function accountable for approving pricing deviations and the sales rep. A sales rep or manager might claim that the pricing policies are keeping him or her from being successful by being too restrictive when, perhaps, more aggressive pricing is needed.

It must be remembered, therefore, that each function in a company provides valuable input for the establishment of pricing parameters. Marketing, for example, should ensure that pricing is oriented to address macro-economic and competitive trends. Marketing often provides advanced competitive analysis for new products, and products that need to be re-positioned. Marketing has a keen eye on competitors' new products, as well as geographic variations when selling globally.

Sales also provides input, but, depending upon the nature of sales incentives, may drive pricing below its optimal levels. Sales, of course, is all about the transaction, and sales management often believes that *every* deal should be won and that it's okay to expect a 100-percent close rate. Often, when a sales team can close more than two-thirds of their deals, it's likely time to consider increasing the price. The pricing function residing in sales makes it difficult for this to happen.

It's very common for a company these days to have an auto-mated pricing tool. By putting in the configuration of the product desired and the customer and location, an algorithm produces a net selling price to propose. This can be effective for companies selling lower-priced products through many transactions. For higher-priced products with fewer transactions, however, it's often best to have a conversation about pricing. The pricing analyst should review the pricing request to ensure the best proposed offering is made versus the competition, and make pricing recommendations accordingly.

Notice that the focus is on pricing versus competition, and not on margins. Getting the highest price from the customer means understanding the competition and offering products at one dollar less for comparable products. Margins are a result of proper competitive positioning as well as a function of product cost, and therefore should not be the driver of setting prices or discounts. If your company's costs are too high, for example, then raising the end user's price to accommodate high costs will mean losing business to competition that might be priced lower. Conversely, if your company's costs are lower than the competitor's, pricing based on margin might mean leaving money on the table.

The degree to which pricing discretion is delegated within a company will drive how efficiently the pricing process will work. Ultimately, while it may be desirable to keep the sales team responsible for their results, both in their close rate and in the resulting pricing level achieved, pricing controlled by a department other than sales can help keep balance in overall economic outcomes.

No matter which department makes pricing decisions, effective pricing decision makers must be aware of relevant competitive alternatives, proper product positioning, and accurate resulting margins to ensure the company is in the best position to win and win profitably.

Contracts

Another important function of operations is contracts. In some companies, the legal department negotiates the contract language, while another function (typically either operations or sales) manages the execution of the contract to ensure compliance and stores it for access when needed. Contract terms must protect the company to be sure that the company is not put at risk. Contract adherence needs to be mandatory. At the same time, contracts should clearly define what is being delivered so that customer expectations are understood.

In several organizations, we had a separate contracts team with legal expertise, but in other cases, the contract liaisons were within our sales operations organization.

Revenue Recognition

In general terms, revenue recognition is an accounting principle that is used to determine the specific conditions under which revenue is recognized or accounted for. There are accounting rules and guidelines that finance adheres to and if these guidelines aren't followed, your wins may not be recognized by the company in the quarter you forecasted—a disastrous result. Revenue recognition guidelines must be anticipated *before* a sale or contract is finalized. Along with finance, operations needs to ensure that sales contracts and terms meet the accounting requirements.

Do's and Don'ts of Revenue Recognition (be sure to consult with your CPA or tax professionals on specifics):

- ☑ Do work closely with legal and finance on contracts.

- ☑ Do put in milestones for services, not completion only.

- ☑ Do ensure your acceptance clauses are reviewed by legal and finance.

- ☒ Do not create side letters; they could impact revenue recognition.

- ☒ Do not put unreleased products and services in contracts; they also could delay revenue recognition.

Internal Company Alignment

Operations is a vital component of the success of the sales team. And just as sales and marketing need to be aligned, it's also important that sales and operations work together as a team. Sales success is a team sport. Long-term success is not achieved by individual mavericks on either the sales teams or the operations teams. All of the successful teams we have been on were tightly aligned between sales and operations—inseparable, in fact! And always remember that collaborative success is easier to replicate!

In Our Experience

Operations is responsible for many important roles in an organization. From our perspective, it is the foundation that keeps sales grounded.

Consider, for example, a sales rep who isn't aware of his revenue recognition guidelines. Suppose, at quarter end, in his haste to get a shipment in for the quarter, he puts a future upgrade on the sales order that represents 60 percent of the deliverable. He has inadvertently just pushed revenue recognition out of the current quarter.

Working together with operations, legal, and finance, we kept our guidelines in check and collectively had to approve every order over a certain size. In several cases, our solutions were in the millions of dollars, so ensuring that we could recognize as much of the revenue as possible in the shortest timeframe was essential for revenue to be recognized in the timeline it was forecasted.

Operations plays a vital role in driving the success of the sales team and meeting the forecasted revenue commitments. When the operations resources are good, they are worth their weight in gold. We've worked with many operations leaders that fit that description. We simply could not have been as successful without their assistance and leadership.

Summary

How to leverage operations to drive MORE sales:

- Forecasting

- Dashboards

- Pricing

- Contracts

- Revenue recognition

- Internal company alignment

The responsibilities that operations fulfills take the burden off the sales reps. Many of these tasks are not ones that many sales reps excel at, or ones for which they have time. Not only do the functions of operations take away from key selling time, but asking sales to perform operations creates a drain on the team, lowering productivity, and ultimately, the overall sales results.

Since creating exceptional customer experience is essential to driving MORE sales, having a top-notch operations team is paramount to your success. The operations team is the foundation that keeps the sales organization functioning and performing at its best. Operations may often be behind the scenes, but it's a critical component enabling the success of any sales organization. Without solid operations, the foundation will crack, if not collapse.

In the next chapter, we'll cover Optimized Sales Processes, another key area in driving MORE sales.

FIVE

Optimized Sales Processes

*"Fifty percent of high-performing sales
organizations (have) sales processes that (are)
closely monitored, strictly enforced, or automated, compared
to just 28% from underperforming sales organizations"*

HARVARD BUSINESS REVIEW[3]

S ales processes are necessary, of course, but they should not be
cumbersome.

---

[3] "What Top Sales Teams Have in Common," Steve W. Martin, *Harvard Business Review*, Jan. 20, 2015.

47

© 2000 Ted Goff

"And then you'll close the sale."

By optimizing your processes, less time can be spent by the sales organization on internal and back office work, thus allowing more time for selling and driving MORE sales. Optimized sales processes can significantly improve the efficiency of working with your prospects and converting them to happy customers. More importantly, improving your processes can have a direct effect on increasing sales velocity, the speed at which a new lead becomes a closed deal.

The ultimate goals of optimized sales processes are:

- *Increased sales velocity,*

- *Repeatable, replicable, predictable results.*

CRM, Pipeline Stages, and Probability

Today, *customer relationship management* (CRM) is a key component in the sales process. CRM is one of the—if not *the*—most fundamental sales tools for helping sales reps manage their customer relationships and progress of each sales opportunity through the sales pipeline. CRM is used to maintain the activity and history of prospects, and to enhance shared knowledge on customer relationships. Used effectively, CRM can be a tremendous tool for sales reps to increase their sales, improve sales effectiveness, and increase their sales cycle velocity. In addition, it allows for management to have shared visibility of all accounts and greater awareness of the critical sales pipeline opportunities and quarterly forecasts.

Five of the top CRM enterprise software solutions are Oracle Siebel, SAP, Salesforce, Microsoft Dynamix CRM, and SugarCRM. But even basic spreadsheets can work so long as they are properly managed and maintained.

There can, however, be drawbacks to CRM. CRM can be a time-sink if not handled properly. For example, having a "full" funnel sounds like a good thing, but it can be misleading. Having unqualified leads in your pipeline is just "stuffing the pipe." The pipeline may look interesting to management, but you'll only be fooling them temporarily, as well as yourself in the process. Pipelines full of inactive opportunities can create false expectations and wasted energy. Each opportunity put into the pipeline needs to be genuine, one that can actively be moved through the various defined stages, progressively becoming more qualified.

Too many sales pipelines are wholly subjective. Often the first thing a new sales leader does is discard his predecessor's list of prospects and start from scratch. For a small company (under $200 million), that means changing sales leaders carries the burden of up to a six-month gap until the sales organization is functioning again.

That said, the only measure of a pipeline is whether it's accurate. If the pipeline predicts a $35 million quarter, was it achieved? If not, has the sales force been adequately trained? Is there forward momentum, a positive trajectory? If not, for a second or third quarter, you need either a new pipeline metric or new sales resources. By the way, a pipeline goal which is regularly exceeded may bring smiles to the management team, but it is no better than a pipeline that is regularly underperforming.

The pipeline is used to forecast your results—against your quota, for the team, to executive management, to your investors, and to the Street if you're a public company. The key is in how you use the data in your pipeline to most effectively project your sales forecast.

To do this, your pipeline should be broken down into sales stages. Optimizing, managing, and minimizing the time spent in each sales stage of the pipeline will allow you to maximize your sales results. By analyzing the time in each stage, you can better understand your funnel's potential for success. It's critical to see where opportunities are getting stalled so that you can then determine what can be done to move them forward. For each sale, the goal is to accelerate progress through the various sales stages and successfully close the opportunity.

The stages and close percentages vary by company and industry, but most include at least these: identification of the suspect, qualifying, proposing, contract, and closing. There can also be other stages added such as product demonstration, proof of concept, and verbal commit.

Stage 1	Identifying	0%
Stage 2	Qualifying	25%
Stage 3	Proposing	50%
Stage 4	Contract negotiations	75%
Stage 5	Close deal	100%

Examples Only

Let's look at each stage and focus on some of the basics.

Identification Process

As we noted in Chapter 1 ("Market"), the first thing is to understand what market you're targeting and what companies fit in your ideal market. Identifying can be as simple as selecting a target list of accounts from all companies that meet your market demographics and "ideal customer profile."

Opportunities at this stage are typically at zero percent probability of close because you're dealing with suspects, not prospects. You only suspect they may have an interest in your product or service and so they're not yet qualified. Do the research now to be sure the suspect list is sound. This will save time later knowing you have your eyes clearly on the right companies.

As an example, we once hired a research group (in India) to investigate our suspect list (multi-million-dollar opportunities) to ensure the suspects met our ideal customer profile. The research group validated the size of the company, defined a need for our solution, identified the economic buyer, identified the influencers, determined the organizational structure, and revealed current competitive suppliers. Outsourcing the research step shortened both the identification stage as well as the qualification stage by months! Naturally we still had to have discussions to validate and further qualify these suspects and prospects, but now we had a foundation of information on which to build and further qualify.

Qualification Process

Of course, the success of your sales force is directly correlated to the *quality* of its leads or prospects. Many salespeople unfortunately waste a tremendous amount of time on leads that are not qualified. Only 25 percent of leads will ultimately close as sales.[4] That means your salespeople can conceivably be spending three-fourths of their time chasing leads that will not bear fruit.

75% of Deals in Sales Pipelines Never Close

"2014 SALES PERFORMANCE OPTIMIZATION STRATEGY,"
ACCENTURE, *CSO INSIGHTS*, 2014

It's important to qualify *in* (and continuously qualify until close) but every bit as important to qualify *out*. Working on an opportunity where there is really no interest or capacity to buy is a waste of time. Does the suspect really have a need for your solution? Is there a pain point? Is a potential solution on their radar? Does the prospect have a budget for this solution? Working on an opportunity that doesn't align with your solution is a waste of time and resources.

Qualification can be the role of sales, marketing, or both. In some cases, sales reps target and qualify customers by directly reaching out to them and focusing on qualifying questions in conversations, workshops, and other information-gathering forums.

In many companies, marketing drives demand generation and passes those leads to sales. Sometimes, however, marketing passes unqualified leads to sales and, in turn, sales reps often don't

---

[4]   According to Gleanster Research

follow up on those leads. A lead might be nothing more than a name—a potential suspect, perhaps, who may have picked up a trinket at a trade show and had someone scan his or her badge. Most salespeople don't have the time to qualify and research leads of this quality because, hopefully, they're focused on better qualified opportunities.

All leads, however, need to be followed up in some manner to determine whether they are qualified, in or out. Marketing can shorten the lead-generation and qualification process with activities such as outreach programs, additional lead generation, and email nurture or drip campaigns. Additionally, marketing can aid by adding the names on a newsletter distribution list, or turning the leads over to market development reps (MDRs), sales development reps (SDRs), or inside sales. Improving the qualification process will drive up sales productivity and conversion rates significantly.

MDRs, SDRs, and Inside Sales

Since we just mentioned them, it might be worthwhile here to take a moment to discuss MDRs, SDRs, and inside sales. Because direct or field sales reps can be an expensive resource to employ to qualify inbound leads, you might want to consider leveraging these potential resources.

The MDR is normally an entry-level sales position and might be tasked with identifying opportunities for the sales reps, perhaps handling and screening inbound inquiries, qualifying or researching them before turning them over to sales. The use of MDRs or telesales is a common way for marketing or sales to generate leads. The key is to ensure those leads are solid enough, actionable, and lead to an actual meeting with a sales rep. Tight integration with the sales team is vital to success. To reduce the gap with field sales, these roles often report to the sales VP rather than marketing.

SDRs can be an alternative, or can perhaps augment the work of the MDRs. Think of the SDR as a sales rep with a more outbound focus than an MDR. An SDR's function might be to make initial contact with a prospect, perhaps working off of a lead list from marketing. The SDR can qualify the prospect at least part of the way into the pipeline before turning the prospect over to a sales rep.

Inside sales can also be an invaluable resource in the qualification process. Customers don't always require a sales rep to meet with them in person. Inside sales comes in many forms today. There are some who qualify opportunities for the sales organization and some who even set appointments. In fact, rather than a typically more expensive outside salesperson, inside sales reps can be the primary sales resource, pushing the sale all the way through the close stage.

Inside sales reps can be quota-carrying, with their own list of accounts. Unlike outside reps, they might focus on companies with a smaller annual transaction size, or prospects or customers with lower overall revenues. However they are used, inside sales reps can be highly successful in converting opportunities to close, and often at a significantly lower cost than outside sales reps.

"Inside sales is growing three times faster than traditional sales."

"INSIDE SALES MARKET SIZE 2013,"
BEN WARNER, INSIDESALES.COM RESEARCH DIVISION

"46% of high-growth tech companies are growing via inside sales."

"THE TREND THAT IS CHANGING SALES,"
HARVARD BUSINESS REVIEW, STEVE W. MARTIN, NOVEMBER 4, 2013

*"An outside sales call costs $308,
an inside sales call costs $50."*

PointClear,
from AAISP 2015 Front Lines Conference

More and more companies are leveraging the inside sales rep approach, in part due to growth in Cloud- and SaaS-based models with lower initial average selling price or ASP. To keep the selling cost down, a lower-cost sales model needed to emerge. As software and marketing tools evolved and improved, customers became more comfortable with phone interaction in place of formal meetings. Demos are now often conducted online without the high cost of travel.

For some companies, inside sales can be a game-changer. But remember, inside sales does not necessarily eliminate the need for outside or direct sales reps. Outside sales is still very important in many industries, particularly in complex solution areas where more involved services or implementations are required, where there are intricate agreements, or where there are high price points. Or— when a strong customer relationship is needed.

Qualifying Questions

There are several options to qualifying your prospects. Software plugins to CRM are available for sales resources to conduct "drip programs," also known as lead nurturing programs, as well as lead scoring to prioritize the best leads to be pursued first. Asking qualifying questions is one of the key methods to prioritizing and qualifying your leads. The most important question you need to ask yourself is whether the company or division is large enough to need—and fund—the purchase. That speaks to the overall size of the IT budget or IT staff. Another question is whether the incumbent is a purchased solution or developed in-house. The latter may be more difficult to displace unless there's been a recent change in the CIO, for example.

Some examples of basic initial qualification questions to ask your prospects:

- What is the business problem you are trying to solve?

- Who is involved in making the decision?

- What is the decision process?

- What is your timeline for having a solution in place?

- Is there a compelling event? Is the project already in your budget?

- Is there an incumbent? Can you describe what was working? Not working? Why are you making a change?

- What are the decision criteria for this opportunity?

It's important to understand that qualification is not a one-time activity. These may be the initial questions, but there will be many more over the course of your relationship with the prospect. Qualification occurs in initial research and over many meetings and discussions. To move your opportunities forward through the sales pipeline, you'll want to continuously qualify your prospects and the best way to do that is to ask the right questions.

If you learn during the qualifying process that the prospect doesn't have the budget for your offering, then move on. Your time will be better spent with a prospect who has a budget and a corporate edict to fix their problem as quickly as possible, rather than with a prospect who's just kicking tires. Moreover, make sure you're talking with a decision maker. If you're not, quickly determine what the next steps are to meet with the decision makers.

If your prospect's needs don't fit with your capabilities, you have no competitive offering, or your prospect has an interest but no budget or compelling event (budget expiration, compliance, audit, current contract expiration, etc.), then you might consider moving the prospect back to marketing or your SDR or MDR to further qualify. This way, you can put the prospect in a nurture or drip campaign to make sure your organization is reaching out to them periodically. Your sales reps should be focused on finding opportunities that have a realistic chance of closing soon. And if there aren't enough qualified leads that can realistically close in the quarter, or year, to meet your quota, then you'll need to find more opportunities.

Once you've determined your prospect is qualified and you're dealing with a decision maker (or decision makers), your qualifying questions should serve to probe for even further information. Probably there are several competitors vying for the sale. You'll need to do a better job than your competitors by better meeting the prospect's objectives and better solving their problems. How do you find out how to do this? Ask! (We know of one sales rep who keeps a yellow post-it note taped on his phone with the word *ASK* written on it. It's a great reminder for all sales reps.)

Your approach should be calculated to ascertain a lot of information with a minimal number of direct questions. Prospects don't want to be grilled. It's a conversation, not a game of twenty questions. Weave your questions into your discussion. Ideally, your questions should be asked of *each* of the decision makers to ensure there is internal alignment at your prospect's company.

The qualification process is often the longest stage because it encompasses many meetings and many conversations with stakeholders of your prospect. As you proceed through the sales process, you want to continuously validate that you are meeting the prospect's timeline and that your solution is aligned with their needs and outcomes. Check to see if there are any gaps, perceived or real. Handle objections quickly. If, for example, one factor in their decision is that their vendor needs to have a location in China and they erroneously believe that you don't have a location there, you won't know that unless you are diligently digging into their objections to properly correct any misconceptions. It's critical that you understand the prospect's decision-making criteria to ensure that they are aware that you meet it.

In addition, you want to ask questions that are trial closes. A trial close is a sales technique where you ask questions to try to determine just how interested the buyer is in your offering and, further, if he's ready to buy. Besides poor qualifying skills, the biggest problem in sales is poor closing skills. By asking your prospects questions, you'll learn a lot about their perspective and where you stand. Here are a few questions to help with qualifying and trial closing:

- Does the solution we've discussed meet your needs?

- What is the next step to move forward?

- Should I send over a copy of our contract for your legal team to start reviewing?

- How do we rank among your final candidates?

- What do we need to do to earn your business, and become your preferred vendor?

- Based on what you've seen and heard so far, is this a fit for what you are looking for?

- Based on what you've seen so far, do you think our offering could be a viable solution for your problem?

- Is there anything you can think of that might stand in the way of us doing business together this quarter?

It's simple really—do your research, and ask good qualifying questions. It's an easy way for your salespeople to stand out above most of your competitors' sales reps. Conversely, not understanding your customers' needs can give your salespeople a reputation of being unprofessional. The more you know about your prospect's specific needs, the better prepared you are to make a proposal that aligns with their expectations. And this will go a long way towards exhibiting your credibility, and earning the prospect's respect.

You want your salespeople to become trusted advisors—people that your prospects know truly understand their business, their industry, the top trends, and issues that are impacting them. Your sales reps can easily be in that upper percentile of sales professionals who understand the needs of the customer. It's not difficult. They just need to do their homework. And ASK!

Proposal Process

How do you present your solution to your prospect? How do you create awareness and a preference for your solution? One large, publicly-traded company we joined had a tool for cranking out pricing. It was a sheet that looked like a bill of materials, lines with words on it with pricing to the right. No messaging, no value proposition, no problems solved, no customer outcomes—in short, no validation that they understood the customer's top issues or decision criteria. Just a single page with numbers on it. That's what the sales reps sent to prospects as their proposal!

What image do you want to portray? Looking professional is minimal table stakes. What's the value to the customer? How do you solve their problems? That's what the proposal needs to convey.

In sales, you're proposing an offering with the intent of closing. The proposal should be a response to the prospect that validates their needs and explains why you have the best solution to meet those needs and solve the prospect's problems. You need to express what your unique differentiation is as a company and the unique solution you offer.

You might also include the top five reasons to go with your solution. You might have some company history that shows your breadth of expertise and differentiation in the industry. (Recall Chapter 2— Messaging.) You want it to be clear, concise, and compelling. You've created awareness; now is the time to create preference. If you have reference customers, they need to be included in your proposal. Try to find ones in the same industry and with the same needs as your prospect. And if they know or respect each other, all the better!

"83% of people trust recommendations from friends and family above all other forms of marketing."

NIELSEN GLOBAL TRUST IN ADVERTISING REPORT RELEASED 9/28/15

Pricing Process

There are two phases in pricing. First, it's important to set a market-driven price based on the current competitive environment. To accomplish this, it's necessary to know your products' perceived benefits and perceived prices, as well as those of your competitors. Why "perceived"? Because it doesn't really matter what *you* may think the product is worth. It only matters how the prospect feels about the product and price relative to the next best alternative. The reality is that any opportunity large enough to warrant a direct sales call will encounter competitive bids. So, the question is, how does your price and product measure up against the opponents? To ferret out this information, you might ASK your prospect. Talk to other customers, ask your resellers, look at other wins and losses from prior opportunities, gather competitive intelligence.

At the intersection of perceived benefits and perceived price is *perceived value*. Setting a market-driven price must reflect the desired perceived value versus your competition. To gain market share and drive more sales, you must have a higher perceived benefit for a comparable perceived price versus your competition, or a lower perceived price for a comparable perceived benefit versus your competition. Oftentimes, increasing the perceived benefits is less costly..

With list prices set, net prices and discounts must be considered for inclusion in the proposal. When a prospect compares the perceived value of your product to the perceived value of the competition's products, they will make trade-offs for what they want most. More features versus lower prices, for example. As the prospect gets closer to making a purchase decision, sales may have the opportunity to shape the customer's perceptions of value. And, they may have the opportunity to adjust and update the specific product features and pricing. A "bid desk" process, the second phase in pricing, can be used to systematically review, adjust, and recommend to sales reps how those trade-offs compare to competition, while management considers resulting margins from those potential changes.

Making deal-specific price changes, either before the proposal is made or during the deal negotiations, is a very delicate and nuanced process. It requires an independent review and consistent analysis so that sales reps avoid selling their own management on reasons designed merely to lower the price. Yet, the final decision must be in the hands of the leadership responsible for delivering the financial results. The bid desk must remain the unbiased (and non-commissioned) neutral party that provides important pricing, value, and margin information.[5]

Contract Process

How long does your contract typically take to be executed? Is it easy for prospects to sign your contracts, or do your contracts end up in extensive negotiations and lots of redlining? Multiple areas of your company may need to get involved in the contract process. There are legal terms such as limitation of liability that legal and finance must consider, financial questions such as payment terms that finance must contemplate, and issues such as leveraging the customer's logo in promotional material that marketing or sales must weigh in on.

What can be done to make your contract less onerous? What can you do to accelerate the contract process? One way to speed things up internally is to identify a list of terms that can be negotiated, and determine by name who has the authorization to negotiate them.

---

[5] For an illuminating discussion of the pricing process, see *The Price Advantage*, by Michael V. Marn, Eric V. Roegner, and Craig C. Zawada (John Wiley & Sons, Inc., 2014).

"This is just our standard 300 page contract. Sign here."

If you know the contract phase is going to take an average of four weeks, factor that into your close process. But, at the same time, look at ways to optimize your contract process. In one of the companies we worked for, we had a very complex multimillion-dollar solution, with a lot of risk and a host of privacy and security concerns. We found that the contract phase alone was taking 90 days on average. So we created a contract task force and we focused on simplifying the contract. Our efforts went towards leveraging best practices, rewriting the contracts, shortening them, taking out onerous language (that we frequently had to negotiate out anyway), and making the contracts more customer-friendly—all while still protecting our company and its valuable intellectual property. The outcome was a greater than 50-percent reduction in contract cycle time. Result: we had time to close more deals, reduce overall resource requirements including legal resources, and focus on creating positive customer experiences.

Closing Process

There are many ways to accelerate the close process. An especially effective one that we touched on in Chapter 3 on metrics, is the implementation of a "close-plan." We'll also discuss close plans in Chapter 12 – Execution. We implemented close-plans at companies that were both large and small. We documented the status of each element of the close plan in our CRM and held regular reviews. The goal of each close-plan was to define any gaps in the closing process, outline required next steps, and align the appropriate company resources necessary to close the proposal.

In some sales, a huge factor in closing a proposal is the strength of your relationship with the prospect. All things being equal, people prefer to buy from trusted friends. Your proposal can be significantly weakened by a strong relationship the prospect has with your competitor. To the extent either you or your management have strong relationships, the close-plan should orchestrate the timing and context for relationship selling. Building a relationship with the prospect takes time. So start early to cultivate relationships that will help you get the win!

As for the close-plan itself, you're going to want to review such areas as:

Decision-makers: Who are the decision-makers and influencers? Do you have all the appropriate contacts? Do you have the appropriate alignment with those contacts?

Desired Outcomes: Do you understand the outcomes your prospect desires? Do you have clarity on the problems and needs they want to address? And how effectively have you communicated that?

Deadlines: Is there a compelling event? Is there a critical date, for example, that the prospect must migrate their mission-critical systems? For example, most retail systems will have to be completed by October to avoid any risk to holiday sales. And manufacturing systems will often have to be installed at least three months before customer acceptance to ensure no production delays. Is a contract about to expire? Is their budget about to be withdrawn? Can you try to create a compelling event, such as time to implementation, or a time-stamped promotion?

Barriers to the close: Sometimes it helps to work it backwards. What needs to be done by what date to close by X date or quarter end? Are there gaps that might put your close at risk? Additionally, what are the risks to meeting those dates? Must the prospect complete a 30-day proof of concept (POC), for example? Do they have an acceptance period? How much time will they need to assess all responses to the RFP? Is there a concern that their decision will be contested and delayed?

Signature authority: Know who has signing authority and what availability they have to sign by week, month, or quarter end. There's nothing more disheartening than thinking or declaring that you're going to close on a certain date, and a week before, you find out the person with signing authority is on a two-week cruise!

Rigorous use of a close-plan approach improves your familiarity with the deal, exposes gaps, and clearly defines a go-forward list of actions. It has the potential to accelerate the close date, increase the close ratio, and make results more predictable. By sharing the insights across the team, you can create replicable, repeatable results. Whether your close plans are complex or very simple, you'll find they are an incredibly effective way to achieve MORE sales.

After the Close

Closing the sale is where a lot of companies stop. But for successful organizations, this is just the beginning.

Making sure that your customers achieve the outcomes for which they purchased your solution should be your next step. And your efforts can't stop there. Delighting your customers should be considered an ongoing process. If you don't maintain a relationship with your customers, you can be assured that your competition will.

Especially in SaaS companies, churn can be a problem. Your goal is to make sure that your customers renew, by providing exceptional service and support. In addition, delighted customers are more likely to be interested in the other solutions you offer, thus expanding your footprint (up-selling and cross-selling your other solutions) to solve their other business problems. Customer satisfaction—better yet, delight—must be paramount. Delighted customers renew, buy more, and provide referrals. We'll talk more about retention and referrals in Chapter 8.

In Our Experience

We've been surprised at the lack of even basic sales processes at several companies. Some had no proposal library. No request for proposal (RFP) library. No standard template cover letter to go with the quote. No systematic pricing review. Everybody just proceeded in their own way. Some proposals were well-written and professional; some were little more than rudimentary quotes attached to emails.

In several companies, the improvements were relatively simple. Our team surveyed the sales force and pooled all the proposals and cover letters that various salespeople were using. After confirming the accuracy and legal compliance of a short list of materials, we picked the most compelling ones—the ones that best represented and differentiated our company and resulted in closed sales. Then we voted on them and sent the combined best proposal materials out as a template for everyone to use. These templates had been battle tested and had stood the test of time.

The important thing was that we made it very much a collaborative effort. Everyone submitted great ideas. The outcome was a proposal template for use by MDRs, SDRs, inside sales, outside or direct sales reps, and our channel partners and resellers—a consistently compelling and professional message to customers. By not having to create a new proposal each time from scratch, we shortened the proposal sales cycle significantly and increased our close rates.

Elements of a Typical Proposal

- Executive Summary
- Objectives and outcomes requested by prospect

- Reasons our solution is the best to meet the prospect's needs
- Unique differentiation
- References in similar industry
- Company highlights and breadth of experience
- Pricing and terms
- Appendix of other offerings

Summary

Key processes to optimize:

- Suspect identification
- Prospect qualification
- Proposal responses and bid desk
- Contract negotiation
- Closing the sale
- Customer delight after the sale
- Renewals, Up-sell, and Cross-sell

A company's sales processes are those stages or processes that a sales rep follows to move a prospect from identification to close—a win or a loss. Optimizing those processes and refining them to make them more efficient and more effective will have a material impact on your sales results.

The result of a successful sales cycle—a won opportunity—is when you deliver the outcome the customer is looking to achieve. Let's look at customer outcomes next.

SIX

Outcome-Based Selling

*"70% of people make purchasing decisions to solve problems.
30% make decisions to gain something."*

IMPACT COMMUNICATIONS

In the past, companies primarily sold based on product features, functions, and benefits. Then the sales profession moved to solution selling, focusing on the problem any given customer was trying to solve, identifying their pain, and working to deliver a "pain-stopping" solution. Now, the selling process has evolved again and today the focus is on something even more significant. Today's sales professional is concerned with a more forward-looking question: what is the *outcome* the customer is striving to achieve?

In this chapter, we'll focus on a vital element towards driving MORE sales: understanding the outcomes that the customer is striving to achieve, knowing how to determine what those outcomes are, and refining your skills to help shape and influence them.

Clarify Desired Customer Outcomes

Outcomes may include simplifying and accelerating processes, enhancing customer relationships, reducing costs, or meeting regulatory requirements. But, while they may seem obvious, some customers are not clear within their own management ranks as to what their company goals are. There can be a lot of potential areas for inquiry, so it's necessary to push the prospect for clarity.

Ultimately, the prospect's objectives need to be clarified with respect to your deliverables. What is the ROI (return on investment)? What is the TCO (total cost of ownership)? What does the RFP (request for proposal) state as the deliverable? What's in the SOW (statement of work), or SLA (service level agreement)? You'll want clear expectations before presenting your solution.

Aligning your Resources

Understand that in the eyes of the customer, both the problem and the desired outcomes are uniquely theirs. Thus, your messaging to them should be focused on how you solve *their* problem, specifically. Your solution has to be presented as one-of-kind for *that* customer. Think of it like this: customers aren't buying your product; they're buying the solution you're offering to meet the outcome they desire. Meeting that outcome is the difference between a satisfied customer and an unsatisfied customer. And operations, sales, services, customer success teams, marketing, and development each have a role to play in meeting the outcome the customer is looking for.

"Can we swap glasses? It helps me see
things from the customer's point of view!"

Outcome-Based Frameworks

An outcome-based framework is a template or guide that outlines the key areas on which to focus when deploying outcome-based selling. There are many frameworks that can be used. At one of the companies we worked for, we created an outcome-based framework for all of our major accounts. The framework identified such areas as:

- Business goals

- Business strategies

- Business initiatives

- IT initiatives

- Key stakeholders

- Key performance indicators

Each of these areas was validated with each large customer to ensure alignment. Further, it was important to confer with several stakeholders of each customer to understand the priorities of the company and confirm that there was internal alignment. As a matter of management discipline, we wouldn't have any subsequent customer meetings regarding any of our offerings without first reviewing our outcome-based framework. The focus was always on addressing the outcomes that were important to customers, and aligning our solutions with the elements defined in the framework.

Define solutions that deliver customer-desired outcomes

Ensuring that Desired Customer Outcomes are Met

In one large software company where we led a global sales team, our operations, sales, services, and customer success teams were all engaged in aligning our solutions to our customers' desired outcomes. We created cross-functional teams to focus on this process. After each customer contract was signed, the customer was assigned a "Customer Success Manager" (CSM). The CSM tracked metrics in support of key performance indicators, often including the achievement of the customer's outcome, the customer's satisfaction with the solution, SLAs, and NPS (net promoter score, which we'll cover in more detail in the next chapters).

Each CSM was available as a key point of contact to gather and report on the customer's issues and concerns. The CSM held formal, quarterly meetings with the customer's key executives, either in person or over video conference, to share their metrics and to hear feedback. Our customer success teams would have the customer rate the company's service and support before or at *each* meeting, and fill out a survey assessment in several areas. Each team's role was ultimately focused on achieving customer outcomes and delivering customer delight.

Each CSM worked on the issues the customer brought to their attention. The goal was to ensure the customer's issues were addressed and resolved before the next meeting, and for the customer to truly feel that they were a top priority. Not surprisingly, the result was that our retention rate was incredibly high.

In another large company, the customer success teams included Customer Account Managers (CAMs). Similarly, they were assigned after the customer contract was signed. The primary difference versus a CSM was that the CAM focused on achieving the contractual service-level agreements in addition to addressing service issues and ensuring ongoing customer delight. The CAMs tracked metrics, uptime, service calls, time-to-resolution, satisfaction ratings, and NPS. They also held formal, quarterly meetings on site. For us, it was a critically important role for services to ensure the highest levels of customer satisfaction.

Focus on achieving customer outcomes, and customer delight.

Consider Using Outcome-Based Pricing

A potential addition to outcome-based sales is outcome-based pricing. This is becoming more common in the outsourcing business where we both worked for many years. Outsourcing is when you use another company to do your services, such as infrastructure technology or managed services. Companies often go to outsourcing suppliers when they have a desire to do such things as

- Lower their labor costs,

- Innovate through third parties,

- Leverage external resources,

- Leverage a global knowledge base,

- Offload non-core capabilities to focus internal resources more strategically,

- Realize a potential for significant cost savings,

- Mitigate or reduce risks.

These are all outcomes that a customer may want to achieve. Oftentimes, outsourcing offerings are priced based on a time-based fixed fee or a cost-based time and materials approach. But the outcome-based pricing model offers another choice. With outcome-based pricing, payment is delayed and occurs only when you have successfully met the desired outcomes, such as reduced costs or increased revenue. Consequently, by tying contracts to specific measurable outcomes, you have more "skin in the game" and a correspondingly higher commitment to delivering on the claims.

Going to an outcome-based pricing structure is a bold move. Before you take the leap, be sure you have deep industry expertise and domain knowledge, as well as a very thorough understanding of your customer through frequent collaboration with them.

A common contractual approach for traditional offerings are service level agreements (SLAs) that focus on the type of services, reporting, reliability, and response times instead of business outcomes. An SLA under an outcome-based pricing model would emphasize alignment with and support of business outcomes.

A great deal of visibility is required to effectively track and measure resulting outcomes. Such a pricing model requires a high level of management and cross-functional commitment. While it can be financially rewarding, it's not without risk. You need to be tightly integrated with your customer and have a high degree of sophistication to successfully carry out this type of pricing. To maximize the combined benefit, both parties need to be committed to mutual success.

Summary

To achieve the best results:

- Focus on important customer outcomes.

- Align your resources around customer outcomes.

- Use an outcome-based framework.

- Ensure that desired customer outcomes are met.

- Recognize the importance of customer success teams.

- Consider outcome-based pricing.

In today's selling environment, the goal needs to be creating exceptional customer experiences. Being focused on the customer's outcomes and solving their business problems is the catalyst for building a successful business and long-lasting relationships.

Of course, before customer relationships can happen, one needs customers in the first place. We've talked about your market and your messaging and the things you need to do to directly optimize your selling efforts. But there's another way to extend your market presence and attract more customers: resellers and partners. Those will be covered in our next chapter.

SEVEN

Resellers and Channel Partners

"Resellers are an essential and viable component of any sales strategy."

STEPHEN POLLACK, INSIDESPIN

Pursuing a reseller or channel partner strategy (sometimes referred to as "indirect" sales) should be a part of your larger go-to-market (GTM) model. The sales strategy flows from the product and marketing strategy. It's important to determine where the channel fits in the bigger strategic context of the company. How does the channel strategy impact your GTM model? How do channel partners impact bringing your product to market, what markets you serve, or what pricing you offer? Resellers and channel partners (collectively referred to as "partners" from here on for simplicity) can be a critical element of the GTM model.

Partners represent a significant way to build and expand market presence and get products to market. How?

- Partners provide more feet on the street at a much lower cost than hiring full-time resources.

- Partners can build solutions that extend your offering.

- Partners can add incremental services that make your solution a better fit for certain customers.

- Partners can enter markets in which they have a foothold that you don't have. Small-medium businesses are good examples. In addition, they can bring value in international markets where they know the customers, the culture, the customs, and the language.

Channel Partner Types

There are several types of partners to consider and in this chapter, we'll focus on the four most important:

1 *Resale partners.* These are distributors and resellers including value-added resellers (VARs) or solution providers (often smaller resellers), systems integrators (SIs), systems manufacturers (sometimes referred to as OEMs), and service providers (this term is often used for telcos).

2 *Technology partners.* Typically, non-resale partners, these are vendors of hardware or software that certify their solutions with your technology.

3 *Alliance partners.* With these partnerships, the relationships are generally strategic and tend to include some financial investment from one or both parties.

4 *Services and consulting partners.* Much like technology partners, but they bring services instead of hardware and software.

Resale partners normally resell an offering as part of a larger solution they offer, typically buying the offering at a discount and then marking it up to sell to the end customer. They may bundle the offer with their own value-add, such as software or services, to make a more complete solution. Resale partners represent a very effective way to build or expand your market presence. The resale partners in software and services are continually evolving, especially with cloud and SaaS, big data, mobile, analytics, and security solutions exploding.

Resale partners include distributors (who sell to others that then resell; e.g., Ingram Micro and Tech Data); value added resellers (VARs) and solution providers (SPs) (like CDW, Presidio, and Fusion Storm who sell to end users); and systems integrators (such as Accenture and CSC who also sell to end users). There's also a type of partner referred to as an agent. Agents act like VARs but don't take title to hardware and software, instead preferring that the vendors sell directly to the end-user. Agents, often called referral partners, aren't especially common in the technology industry.

> *"Two thirds of all computing sales in the world
> are not direct sales ... instead, they are
> 'Channel Sales' or 'Indirect Sales.'"*
>
> ANDY DICKENS, VIRTUAL SALES, LTD

Technology partners typically certify their solutions to work with, or on, another offering. Technology partners may be other software or hardware companies who certify their solutions on your platform, or vice-versa. Typically, technology partners sell their offers independently.

A good example of a technology partnership is VMware's Technology Alliance Partner Program. This program provides the tools and resources for software and hardware companies to test, integrate, package, and certify their solutions with VMware offerings. They have several Alliance tiers that offer different benefits such as webinar collaboration, access to product managers, joint press releases, joint white papers, and inclusion in partner listings. On SAP's website, they promote to prospective partners exclusive online access to partner-only sales and marketing tools, events, solution information, support, demos, education, benefits, and more. These technology partnerships benefit these companies by expanding their brand awareness, extending offerings on their platforms, and facilitating software and hardware providers to leverage their brands and market presence.

Alliance partnerships can involve two or more companies working together in a relationship that is typically more strategic than a technology partnership. Normally there's a greater investment in engineering, marketing, services, and sales involvement between the companies.

With alliance partners, each may have a proven solution. But when a customer makes use of the technologies of both, such as a server platform from HP and an ERP solution from SAP or Oracle, the customer typically benefits by the combination. Sometimes with alliance partners, there will be joint marketing plans, joint engineering plans, joint sales models, and joint service and support plans. Together, as alliance partners, there may be opportunities to expand the solutions' capabilities, create a new market, or extend into a new vertical segment. Each vendor typically sells their solution independently, but may also promote the benefits of how the offerings work together.

Services and consulting partners include such categories as managed service providers (MSPs), cloud service providers (CSPs), and consultancies. These partnerships focus on services. As technology gets more complex, services such as remote management of client IT systems, network management, security, email, desktop and mobile devices, cloud, virtualization, as well as many other services will continue to increase in demand. Examples of MSPs include Accent Computer Solutions, Computer Resources of America, and Network Data Systems, among many others. A cloud service provider is a company that provides an element of cloud computing, such as Software as a Service (SaaS), Platform as a Service (PaaS), or Infrastructure as a Service (IaaS). CSP examples include Amazon Web Services, Google Cloud, and Microsoft Azure. Consultancies include large well-known firms like KPMG, PWC, CSC, and Accenture, as well as smaller regional companies.

Regardless of the category of the partner, there's a common misperception that you can just flip a switch and your partners will magically make your solution sell.

Rules of Engagement

It's very important to define how you and your team will work with your partners. Do you want them to focus on a territory? A certain vertical segment? Accounts of a certain size? Named accounts? The better defined the approach and expectations, the better the chances for success (and the less chance of conflict or miscommunication). In your rules of engagement (usually a working document and not part of the formal agreement), define the segments, how to register deals, and how you want to work together as partners. And then communicate these rules internally and externally. The more specific you can be in outlining your vision with your partners and the clearer you can be with the partner-specific rules of engagement, the better your relationships with your partners will be and the less productivity-stealing ambiguity you'll experience.

If the partner doesn't receive clear information on your strategy, the business model, and engagement model, and if they don't see a clear commitment to mutual success, you'll be opening the door for concern, confusion, and conflict. Also, you're going to need to show your partners how your product or service is sold. You'll need to share success stories and case studies with them, and create new success stories with joint reference customers. Overall, you'll need to share your best ideas with your partners so that they can drive more sales for you.

> *"IT vendors can build revenue or slide into fiscal failure, depending on how they manage the channels in which they do business. To succeed, vendors must embrace best practices in channel management and break bad habits."*

> MICHAEL HAINES, ALAN MACNEELA,
> "BEST AND WORST PRACTICES FOR IT CHANNEL PROGRAMS,"
> GARTNER RESEARCH

Alignment at Both the Executive and Field Levels

Formalizing a strategic agreement, complete with a jointly developed and agreed-upon GTM plan, with alignment at the executive level, is imperative before embarking on a partner strategy. Once that alignment is in place, then it's essential that you have executive engagement between your companies (you and the partner) to monitor and measure success. The daily execution typically occurs in the field, so a tight alignment between local management is also important for sustainable channel success.

Market Presence

Embarking on a partner strategy generally requires market presence. Your partners won't typically create your initial market for you. So, you'll need to have proof points; your solution must meet a need in the market, and have a unique advantage.

This is an untapped market.. Want to be our first reseller?

Signing up early adopters and establishing market acceptance come under the role of the vendor, not the partner. The more references and industry kudos you have, the better. If yours is not a solution that sells easily, nor has a competitive advantage, the partner will likely gravitate to another vendor in their portfolio that attracts greater market interest.

Agreements

The greater clarity achieved in the agreement, the less potential there is for misalignment or channel conflict down the road. It's common practice to separate the resale agreements from the policy documents and guidelines. The latter can be easily updated as required. Because of ever-changing market conditions and competitive threats, make sure the partner agreements are easy to change. Not every relation-ship adjustment will require an agreement change. Above all else, just be sure that the agreements are win-win arrangements for both parties.

Demand and Lead Generation Programs

When you start a partner relationship, it's usually necessary to prime the pump and build demand. Vendors need to create the market.

Partners can't be expected to do that in their role and with their margins. Work together with the partner to jointly win the first one, two, or more accounts. Build some early success stories. Those success stories can then be leveraged as the "how" to win subsequent deals. With some partners, you'll need to be engaged in all oppor-tunities. With others, after a few joint opportunities, you'll have "taught them to fish" and they'll pursue additional opportunities with minimal support.

Partners can benefit from demand and lead generation oppor-tunities such as inbound leads, trade show leads, and outbound campaigns to continue to prime the pump.

Programs are important to drive awareness, preference, and loyalty. Some partners will require an investment, such as market development funds (MDF) and resource commitments. Bonuses and contests can also help drive focus on selling your solutions.

Essential Sales Tools

You wouldn't expect your sales reps to come on board and imme-diately know your elevator pitch, your tag line, your qualifying questions, your unique differentiated message, and how you're better than the competition. The same holds true for partners. They'll need the best of the best sales tools to accelerate their successful selling efforts with your solution. We'll cover essential sales tools in greater detail in Chapter 11.

Deal Registration, Partner Relationship Management

You may want all the partner deals to be registered through a deal or opportunity registration program. This helps ensure that a channel partner is protected if they create a deal so that nobody can successfully poach it. You'll need to have systems to manage this, which requires an investment.

There are costs, and efforts, to build channel IT and infrastructure. Often the investment is SaaS based and tied to an ERP and CRM system. There's an exploding market to enable vendors and partners in this area. Partner Relationship Management (PRM), for example, includes software tools to enable vendors to more effectively manage their partner relationships. The software modules include tools such as partner portals, deal registration portals, content management, partner and customer contact databases, pricing, and online product and skills training.

Enablement

Your partners need your help to be successful. Whether it's onboarding, product training, software development kits (SDK), technical or engineering support, or skills training, it's your organization's responsibility to ensure your partners have what they need. You'll need to provide a field team—channel managers, solutions engineers, and inside or direct sales reps—that are armed with the resources your partners need to succeed. The better you enable your partners, the better the outcomes. (Look for more on enablement in Chapter 10.)

A critical success factor to engaging your partners to drive more partner sales, is for channel reps to receive commissions *and* quota credit for selling your product. And even then, progress will be slow as the channel reps may continue to sell what they know and can close the fastest.

Channel Neutrality versus Channel Conflict

This is the single, most pivotal issue in a partner program, and landing on the right side of it is the difference between the success of the program and failure. At the heart of the matter lies channel-neutral compensation. In policy and in practice, your partners need to experience a channel-neutral compensation environment. It doesn't have to be more favorable to partners, but it must be at least neutral.

Channel neutral compensation is table stakes, and is surprisingly limited in its implementation in the current high-tech world. It used to be more common in technology hardware companies. More recently, however, we've seen many software and SaaS companies struggling in this area. If a direct rep believes he'll receive more commission if he takes a deal direct, rather than through the channel partner, it could cause undesirable behavior, incenting the sales rep to resort to poor practices, like undercutting the partner's price to induce the customer to go direct.

In our experience, facing these possibilities, we've delayed launching partner programs until the compensation was properly modified. Trying to drive a new partner program without the right compensation can create long-lasting damage to partner relationships or the overall channel partner strategy.

The areas to manage, however, are greater than simply a compensation plan. The key to success is managing channel conflict in general. What will you do if—more precisely, when—the two parties don't see eye to eye? Channel conflict is bound to happen. Prepare for mitigating it in advance. Define clear rules of engagement. How you'll handle channel conflict should be a part of your plan. Otherwise, when conflict happens, it could lead to dissatisfaction from your partners and even the demise of your relationships with them.

Consider these scenarios:

- How will you handle a situation where a partner is working on an account and the direct rep decides to take the opportunity direct, cutting out the partner?

- What will you do if the direct rep decides to push out a partner because he or she receives greater commissions if the partner is not involved?

- What will be your solution to a conflict created when a direct rep decides to significantly undercut the price that a partner can sell your solution for, again effectively cutting out the partner?

- How will you handle a situation where one partner created the lead, and the direct rep brings in another partner?

How will your management respond to these not-uncommon situations?

Scenarios like the above are why there must be alignment between the company's executives and the partner's executives. You simply must have policies in place for when channel conflict is encountered.

We've seen entire programs rendered ineffective because of one bad experience by a sales rep in the field. When it happens, senior leadership typically needs to get involved, with assurances made to their counterparts that the conflict will be handled to each party's satisfaction, and further assurances that such a conflict will never happen again. It's important to remember that the repair in the field sometimes takes longer, as bad experiences travel faster than good ones. So keep a watchful eye. Remember the rules of engagement.

Trust is important in all business relationships but particularly so with partners. Unfortunately, there has been a long history of bad practices across the technology industry. Focus on trust, integrity, and lots of open communications. To avoid the negative effects of channel conflict:

- Ensure your executive management and your sales teams are committed to the partner strategy,

- Maintain channel-neutral policies,

- Take a strong hand against channel conflict,

- Remember that trust and integrity at all levels and across all teams is mandatory.

In Our Experience

Over the years, we've managed many different partners— including distributors, VARs, solution and service providers, MSPs, CSPs, SIs, you name it. We've also managed many alliance and technology partners where our combined product offering was more complete than what could have come from internal sources alone.

In one circumstance of setting up a national partner program, each of our sales reps developed territory or named account plans. Essentially, they owned the plan and were expected to manage it as a business. Their plans were submitted and regularly reviewed. We shared them, so each of the sales reps could learn from his or her peers.

We also developed training (enablement) and sales tools for our partners. It was unrealistic to expect a partner to read all our materials the way our own employees would. The partners, after all, represented many different vendors at the same time. And so they needed us to distill the avalanche of materials— identifying the best of the best sales tools. Because our partners worked with other vendors, the key for us was to rise above the others and to put together a partnership that would yield better results than their other partnerships. We accomplished this by being easier to do business with, by creating better business models, by demonstrating more loyalty, and by establishing a more profitable overall relationship.

In this situation, it was decided to assign our partner reps to our partner's geographic locations. Our partners loved receiving leads from us, but were reluctant to share their customer base. They needed us to go first. We conducted "lunch and learns" to teach them the highlights of our products, but also to enhance face time and to engage in relationship-building. We went on joint sales calls and led the customer discussions when requested.

We surveyed our partners regularly, both informally and formally. What were our competitors doing well? What could we do better? We participated in contests to ensure we were always visible. We conducted reviews at the branch level with management, and we conducted regular national reviews with the national management. We made sure we were tightly linked at all levels. It was essential for us to treat our partners like gold. They each had a wide network and to tap into it, we knew we had to earn the right.

To accelerate our readiness for partnership relationships, we quickly focused on creating compelling success stories. We started with a few pilot accounts, turned them into success stories, and then promoted them widely.

After having managed several global partner relationships, we learned the following principles:

- Corporate partnership commitments start at the top.

- Local or branch partnership commitments are essential.

- Enablement and training play a critical role.

- Crisp, clear, and compelling selling tools are must-haves.

- Don't expect your partners to simply hand over their account bases; build their trust first.

- Making joint sales calls with prospects and customers is a privilege that must be earned; joint account planning can help facilitate working together.

- You must be present to win, and, to be ready to win, you have to work at it.

Summary

To benefit from your resellers and channel partner programs

- Establish clear rules of engagement,

- Establish executive relationships as well as field relationships with ownership and accountability,

- Create the initial market presence,

- Ensure your agreements are win-win,

- Develop lead generation programs,

- Create sales tools that keep things simple and differentiated,

- Institute deal or lead registration,

- Ensure channel neutrality and manage channel conflict.

Resale partners, technology partners, alliance partners, or services and consulting partners can have an extraordinary impact on expanding your brand and your market coverage by putting more feet on the street and creating more resources to tout your solution. Having partners can take more effort, but they are, if managed properly, an incredible sales force multiplier.

EIGHT

Retention and Referrals

*"The key is to set realistic customer expectations,
and then not to just meet them, but to exceed them—
preferably in unexpected and helpful ways."*

RICHARD BRANSON

Retention

How important to your sales efforts is the retention of your existing customers? According to Gartner Group, on average, 80 percent of a company's future profits come from just 20 percent of its existing customer base. Do you know which customers comprise your 20 percent? And are you going out of your way to ensure a satisfying— better yet, *extraordinary*—customer experience? If so, you're in the minority. The typical American business loses half of its customers every five years. Why? Two-thirds of those lost cite inadequate customer care as the main reason.

© 2011 Ted Goff www.tedgoff.com

"Don't worry. I'll call Tech Support, get right through, tell them our problem in ten seconds and they'll have a solution immediately."

Worse, 91 percent of small businesses do *nothing* to retain their existing customers.[6]

Here are a few more revealing statistics to further drive home the point:

- Increasing customer retention rates by just 5 percent increases profits to anywhere between *25 and 95 percent.*[7]

- It costs *five times* more to acquire new customers than it does to keep current ones.[8]

---

[6] *Harvard Business Review*

[7] "Zero Defections: Quality Comes to Services," *Harvard Business Review*, September-October 1990.

[8] "B2B Customer Experience Priorities In An Economic Downturn: Key Customer Usability Initiatives in A Soft Economy," Alan E. Webber, Forrester Research, February 19, 2008.

- The probability of selling to an existing customer is *60 to 70 percent*. The probability of selling to a new prospect is *5 to 20 percent*.[9]

- *Ninety-one percent* of unhappy customers will not willingly do business again with the organization they're unhappy with. Disturbingly, for every customer complaint, there are *26* other dissatisfied customers who remain silent.[10]

- Close to *70 percent* of the identifiable reasons why customers leave companies has nothing to do with the product. The main reason? Poor quality of service.[11]

That last one is interesting because businesses only attribute *21 percent* of customer churn to poor customer service.[12] That's quite a disconnect.

© 1999 Ted Goff

"Can we get past all these complaints to the part where you reorder?"

---

9   *Marketing Metrics*, Neil T. Bendle, Paul W. Farris, Phillip E. Pfeifer (Pearson FT Press, 2015).

10   Lee Resources, Inc

11   Forum Corporation research

12   RightNow Technologies

Furthermore, it shouldn't come as a surprise that in addition to the profitability of retaining happy customers, doing so also leads to greater profitability in the form of referral customers, word-of-mouth advertising, and glowing reviews.

There are several ways to retain customers, including:

Providing Superior Service

- Focus on providing extraordinary support to your customers, make your specific buyer (and potential referral) look good, and avoid any career risk to that individual.

- Ensure that your solutions are meeting the outcomes desired by your customers; confirm with them that the implementation went as promised in the proposal, and make sure that subsequent SLAs are being met.

- Understand your customer's business, and provide new services to meet new requirements.

Focusing on Feedback

- Staying in frequent contact with customers, showing them that you value them.

- Conduct regular reviews to track their satisfaction and feedback.

- Listen for customer feedback via customer surveys and make sure your customers know you are addressing their feedback.

- Measure your net promoter score (NPS) and make it a metric your sales team takes ownership of, thereby taking actions visible to your customers.

Setting up a Customer-Centric Organization

- Create two sales teams—for example, hunters (who go after new accounts) and farmers (who manage and grow existing accounts), to keep engagement with customers high.

- Put major account managers on your top accounts to ensure the focus those accounts deserve.

- Put customer success teams in place to maintain a close relationship with your customers after the initial sale.

Creating Loyalty Programs

- Create VIP rewards program and loyalty member points.

- Create events for top customers with distinguished speakers or industry pundits, or sports events.

- Automatically send out marketing messages and promotions to specific customers.

You've probably seen the promotions cable or internet providers offer to keep customers hooked into contracts to ensure their retention for at least the term of the promotion. And when that promotion expires, there's often another promotion the provider offers to make certain their customers remain captive. This can be very effective with commercial (B2B) customers, as well. Offering bundles and price promotions and focusing on up-sell and cross-sell opportunities are effective ways to keep your customer consistently linked to your solutions across a wider range of services.

Customer Success Teams

Because of the vital nature of retaining customers and ensuring predictable deferred revenue streams, particularly in a SaaS model, more companies are adding "customer account" or "customer success" teams. These teams are responsible for ensuring satisfied customers and, in some cases, responsible for renewals, upgrades, up-selling, and cross-selling. Some companies put customer account teams in services, some in operations, and some put customer success teams in sales. When customer success teams are in sales, companies may assign a quota to the CSM or CAM that's aligned with the given customer. Many companies, however, don't give quotas to these reps, feeling that doing so taints them in terms of providing service. You'll have to decide based on your circumstances what's best for your organization.

The customer success manager's (CSM's) role is to focus on retention and delighting the customer after the initial sale is made. In many companies, the sales rep closes a deal, but then moves on to the next deal to meet his or her quota. The CSM is then assigned to the account to provide post-sales support and to stay actively engaged with the customer throughout the relationship.

CSMs focus on building lasting and consultative relationships with customer accounts. They concentrate on helping customers achieve their business outcomes. And they focus on customer feedback, based on either customer satisfaction surveys or net promoter scores (NPS) (or both).

In fact, there are many responsibilities that fall under the role of CSM. Some CSMs are involved with customers in their day-to-day activities to help them drive best practices, helping them determine what's working and what's not, thus enabling the customer to get the most value out of their solution.

You should be delighting your customers all throughout your company. How customer-friendly and effective are your chat or hotline personnel? Your onsite technicians? *Everyone* makes an impression on customers, especially when a customer is dissatisfied with an issue. Ensuring that everyone is measured on customer delight and retention is a major key towards making it a part of your company's culture. In addition to delighting customers, reducing churn (customer attrition) should be a top priority.

In Our Experience

At many of the Fortune companies where we worked, we had major account teams assigned to one or just a few key accounts. In addition, we had special teams that maintained ongoing relationships with customers. Certainly, the salespeople stayed involved, but the sales reps were often focused on new pursuits to meet their quotas. A CSM or CAM, or "advocate," was assigned to a given account and was measured on how well he or she, along with the entire company, satisfied the customer.

The CSM/CAM tracked many items including NPS, outages, uptime, service calls, and resolution times, in addition to tracking how well the company was doing in sales, marketing, product solutions, services, onboarding, usage, and ROI.

For many cloud and SaaS solution companies, which may in some cases have low switching costs, ensuring customer delight is even more important. Remember (according to the statistics) what it took to acquire those customers of yours: five times the effort it takes to keep them. Never forget the opportunity your customers offer— through up-selling, cross-selling, upgrading, referrals, recommendations—versus the costs of acquiring new customers.

© 1996 Ted Goff

Referrals

"Picture a sales world where you will only be meeting clients who want to meet with you—a world in which you'll never have to cold call again, send prospecting letters, or entice clients with special offers. Enter the world of referral selling."

JOANNE S. BLACK, NO MORE COLD CALLING: THE BREAKTHROUGH SYSTEM THAT WILL LEAVE YOUR COMPETITION IN THE DUST (BUSINESS PLUS, 2006)

Referrals are critical for gaining new customers. Satisfied customers provide referrals and referrals have a higher retention rate. According to a study, referred customers are both more profitable and loyal than non-referred customers.[13] Referred customers had a higher retention rate, a higher contribution margin, and were simply more valuable in both the short and long run. And 76 percent of buyers prefer to talk to vendors recommended by someone they know.[14]

According to Joanne Black, a leading authority on referral selling, salespeople tell her that referral selling has a minimum of a 50-percent conversion rate, with many of them reporting up to 70- to 90-percent conversion. Referrals can happen spontaneously, of course, but successful salespeople don't wait. They cultivate their client relationships and ask for and receive introductions to other ideal prospects. Black notes tha*t smart* referral tactics lead to higher conversion and deeper client relationships.

*"91% of customers say they'd give a referral.
Only 11% of salespeople ask for referrals."*

DALE CARNEGIE

---

[13]   A study conducted by the Goethe University of Frankfurt.
[14]   A study by the market intelligence firm IDC.

"65% of a company's new business is from referrals."

NEW YORK TIMES

Ways to Build up Your Referrals:

- Ask your customers to introduce you.

- Create a disciplined referral program with the appropriate skills training.

- Establish internal referral metrics that drive accountability for results.

- Make referrals a component of your qualitative compensation plans.

- Make it a daily activity: *ask!*

- Create a library of positive references.

Summary

Customer retention and referrals should be the focus of every company, small or large.

Retention

- Provide superior service.

- Focus on feedback.

- Set up a customer-centric organization.

- Create loyalty programs.

Referrals

- Establish internal referral metrics.

- Make referrals a component of your qualitative compensation plans.

- Make it a daily activity—*ASK!*

Customer retention and creating extraordinary experiences for customers are not only how you can differentiate yourself from the competition, they are how you can maintain and grow your company. Creating extraordinary customer experiences is table stakes in this new digital marketing and social media marketplace. Referrals can be the best source of new prospects and loyal customers.

NINE

Rewards and Recognition

"Whether you're a CEO or a VP of sales,
the sales compensation plan is probably
the most powerful tool you have."

MARK ROBERGE, HARVARD BUSINESS SCHOOL

More than most other functional roles in business, professional sales reps are recognized for their achievement of very specific, quantitative objectives (e.g., quotas), and typically rewarded in the form of commissions. Properly motivating and propelling sales reps towards greater success can come both from direct compensation and by publicly celebrating their successes.

Commissions for salespeople typically represent one of the greatest expenses to a company's SG&A (sales, general, and administrative) expenses. With incentives being such a significant cost to a company, it's important to make certain that they are designed to be as effective as they can be in driving the behaviors and the results desired.

Driving MORE sales is the focus of most companies. Rewards and recognition costs can be considered money well spent when they drive the right behavior and lead to the right results. If, however, your rewards and recognition are not properly aligned and sales don't increase as desired, unjustified SG&A costs could well drive the overall profits of your company down, not to mention the lowered profits due to the lack of sales. It's a double hit.

Let's say, for example, that your sales reps are on a 50/50 commission plan, meaning a compensation structure of 50-percent base salary and 50-percent commissions (percentage of targeted earnings potential). The base pay is essentially a fixed cost; the commission pay is variable. Your goal, naturally, is for your sales reps to sell equal to or greater than their respective sales quotas. Sometimes, accelerators are paid for exceeding quota. But if your accelerators for overachievement are too rich, the resulting costs may exceed your compensation budget. To increase the challenge, the extra cost for the overachievers can be greater than the avoided cost for commissions not paid on missed revenue from the underachievers. It's a balancing act, to drive more sales across the group in aggregate while keeping within your cost budget. The goal is for your incentives to be properly *aligned* to create the behaviors you want.

Commission plans have an impact on cost but they also affect personnel retention. According to a recent study, median voluntary turnover was at 10.7% among 240 US technology firms.[15] A sales rep retention problem leads to more pressure on hiring. While companies and environments are different, it's important to consider the impact. For example:

---

[15]   Barton, Scott, "When is it Time to Get Worried about High Sales Force Turnover?", Radford, Web, April, 2015

- What are the characteristics of a great rep? Consider traits such as proven track record, solid history of exceeding quota, passion, and enthusiasm.

- What methods or tests work best in identifying candidates with the greatest potential? Personality tests such as Myers Briggs, Strengths Finder (from Gallup), and The Predictive Index are just a few assessments that are available.

- Is it better to hire experienced reps or train new ones yourself? One consideration is to look at your competitors for their best practices.

Several important catalysts for impacting the retention of sales reps include not only offering competitive products, but very importantly having competitive pay, rewards, and recognition that help to motivate and retain your best sales professionals.

"One study found that the top twenty percent of these "recognition rich" companies have a thirty-one percent lower voluntary turnover rate, a huge measure of performance."

THE STATE OF EMPLOYEE RECOGNITION IN 2012,
BERSIN & ASSOCIATES

There are many forms of rewards and recognition in sales organizations. The most common include commissions; incentives based on key performance indicators (KPIs), management by objectives (MBOs), and sales management objectives (SMOs); new account bonuses; sales contests; sales performance incentive funds (SPIFs); and sales achievement clubs.

"60%: the amount of reps who achieve quota."

CSO INSIGHTS

Quantitative Commissions

Commissions typically represent compensation paid on closed sales. They vary dramatically by industry and by such factors as size of transaction or type of product. Quotas, often a monthly, quarterly, or annual dollar target amount, can further vary based on market factors, as well as the margins associated with the solution.

By paying on total contract value (TCV), for instance, you'll need to consider how to compensate for, say, a one-year contract versus a three-year contract. You might pay a commission for a three-year contract in the first year, which might be a significant expense in that year. Consequently, you might be tempted to structure your pay system based on one-year contracts. But certainly, this would incent the sales reps to drive only one-year contracts rather than three. That could bring greater risk to your company because each one-year contract would need to be "re-sold" each year, with a new round of competition, and maybe even by a new rep who doesn't have the same relationship with the customer. Much can happen in a year. You might even be up against your previous sales rep who moved to the competition because he was dissatisfied with your uncompetitive compensation plan!

You may decide to pay commissions on first fiscal year revenue (FFYR) versus TCV. FFYR refers to the amount of revenue recognized in the first fiscal or calendar year versus the total value of the contract. In this approach, the expense and revenues would more closely align in the same year. How will sales reps respond to selling the deal in November for two months of revenue credit, versus waiting until January and getting twelve months of revenue credit?

Compensation can clearly get complicated. To simplify it, remember the fundamentals. What behaviors are you trying to drive? Test or model different scenarios to see if the results align with your objectives.

Remember as well that the establishment of both the quota and the commission plans must be coordinated with other departments (e.g., operations, legal, human relations, finance) to ensure the plans are profitable, manageable, and scalable. Involving operations and finance is crucial, especially early in the process. Regardless of your solution, your company size, or target market, you want to keep it simple.

Often companies put accelerators in place for achieving over 100 percent. You might also pay an accelerator on strategic solutions, a new offering, a new service, or a high-value reference company. For example, the accelerator might be 1.5 times the percentage, or maybe 2 times the percentage. Instead of $1,000 per percentage point of quota, the rep would receive $1,500 or $2,000 in commissions per percentage sold for the desired result.

We've worked for a few companies where the compensation plans were so complicated, reps simply couldn't figure them out. Ultimately, the reps just did their own thing. The comp plan did little to incent them. It was not a motivator, and it didn't drive the behaviors desired by the company. In fact, in some cases, comp plans are the cause of *de*-motivation.

Revenue quotas, for example, are typically disincentives in services and SaaS businesses. In these businesses, revenue is typically recognized ratably throughout the term of the contract which means revenue recognition occurs month to month as services are delivered. Think about where you want your reps spending their energy, and the resulting financial impact to themselves and to the company. Winning a bigger deal, and winning it this year versus next, has benefits for the company and compensation plans should take that into consideration. Don't create a compensation plan that causes reps to consider a smaller contract, or holding the deal until a month that pays them more.

SaaS revenue recognition is a big deal especially for a company in the process of switching from traditional perpetual license sales. To start, SaaS revenues must be recognized over the life of the relationship with the revenue backlog reflected as deferred revenue. Sales commissions generally get paid at contract signing. But that could cause a significant expense/revenue mismatch. Alternatively, paying commissions over the life of the relationship can cause considerable discomfort among the reps accustomed to speedier payments. In fact, many reps find it impossible to make the switch.

Some companies pay commissions on the annual recurring revenue (ARR) and some pay on the monthly recurring revenue (MRR), which might mean either paying the sales rep MRR based only on the first month of the agreement, or paying for each occurrence of the monthly revenue monthly. Usually, it's better to align the recognized revenue timing to commission payment timing. Whichever way commissions are paid, quotas must be aligned appropriately. For example, if you pay on MRR, your quotas are significantly less versus annual recurring revenue and potentially significantly less than total contract value. TCV, FFYR, MRR, ARR, and even contribution margin (CM) are just a few examples of ways to measure your sales results, and by no means the only options.

As you can see, compensation is not for the faint of heart. Commissions are very personal to sales reps, so you need to make sure you give the commission plan due consideration to make it right for all parties. We've written and released a significant number of new compensation plans to adjust for prior issues and motivate the right sales behavior, in easy to understand terms. The result: we drove MORE sales.

Qualitative Commission Plans

In addition to commission plans, there are many qualitative incentive and rewards options to drive the desired behaviors and outcomes of your sales teams. You may consider using key performance indicators (KPIs), management by objectives (MBOs), or sales management objectives (SMOs).

In start-up sales organizations, new sales can take a while. Therefore, you may want to incent your sales teams to engage in those activities that will help build the foundation of your business.

This means paying for specific activities that you believe will result in creating awareness, preference, and, ultimately, sales. Qualitative plans can be effective in this regard. You might pay MBOs for activities such as pilots, proof of concepts, seminars, demand creation webinars, or meetings at the VP level and above in targeted accounts. None of these, of course, are guaranteed to drive revenue in the short term. But they all will drive awareness and preference on the road to revenues.

Motivate your sales team during the early stages and encourage them to learn from each customer interaction. After there is a proven solution, and it's possible to set realistic quotas, consider converting those qualitative compensation plans to more of a quantitative quota-based system. Or, you might combine them in some way. You might have 75 percent of the incentive plan based on quotas, for instance, and the other 25 percent based on MBOs, or vice versa.

For a successful company, it's not only critical that they close new contracts, but that they retain their current customers. You might consider measuring reps based on follow-on sales and renewals (of maintenance and SaaS) which in some cases are not included in commissions even though they are vital indicators of the health of the company and the stability of its customer base. In addition, qualitative plans may include measuring customer satisfaction through surveys, or, perhaps, be based on customer net promoter scores (NPS).[16] Essentially, an NPS is a rating by a customer (typically on a scale of 0 to 10) on how likely the customer would be to recommend your company to a friend or colleague. Both NPS and customer satisfaction surveys are important measurements of customer delight and highly suitable factors, therefore, on which to base qualitative plans.

---

[16] The NPS metric was introduced by Fred Reichheld in "One Number You Need to Grow," *Harvard Business Review* (2003) and developed by Bain & Company and Satmetrix Systems.

Other examples of what qualitative plans you might track and reward for include:

- Hiring key open sales positions

- Training sales reps on new solutions

- Training sales reps on outcome and value-based selling

- Forecasting accuracy

- Achieving quarterly linearity, thereby avoiding the "hockey stick" phenomenon so prevalent in sales

New Account Bonuses

If gaining new accounts is a key focus for your company, you might consider installing a new account bonus program, either in the commission plan or as a separate program. At one company, we had salespeople write up their success story to be eligible for the bonus. It was a simple form that included:

- Company name and industry

- The problem the customer was trying to solve

- The solution we offered

- The outcome(s)

- The competition

- The winning sales strategy and why they won

Nothing elaborate. The focus was on having a means by which the sales reps could share and leverage their selling experiences amongst their peers (in advance of case studies being created by marketing), and increase the chances of repeating those successes in other accounts.

Sales Wins and All Hands Recognition

A great sales environment is one that celebrates success. In best-practice companies, we held monthly "All Hands" sales calls. In those calls, we recognized the wins of the month and everyone who contributed to those successes. We didn't recognize only the sales reps, but included the solution or field engineers, the contracts group, and whoever else was involved.

Sales Contests

We've created and been involved in many great sales contests. Prizes included cars and trips. One salesperson we worked with won a Miata while another won a Maserati. Contests should be designed so that many plan participants can win, rather than just having one first-place recipient. We had cruises, trips to Hawaii, trips to the Caribbean, and even a trip to Singapore. Trips tend to be great motivators, especially if you include significant others, rewarding them as well for the long and crazy hours the sales reps often must spend away from home while closing MORE sales. Experiential rewards generally provide a better ROI than monetary rewards. Experiential rewards tend to be collaborative in nature, memorable over a longer time, and can accelerate relationships that otherwise may take years to develop.

SPIFs (sales performance incentive funds) are sales contests designed to drive a specific action, typically targeted at short-term goals and provided as bonuses, perhaps for quarterly contests. But of course SPIFs can be applied to longer-term objectives as well.

Sales Clubs

Sales clubs can go by many names—President's Club, Century Point Club, 100% Club, Heavy Hitter's Club, Chairman's Club, The

Winner's Circle, and so forth. Typically, gaining "membership" to the club means achieving more than 100 percent of annual quota. In addition to a fun trip for the sales rep and their significant other, the status the club itself confers is often worthy of pursuit.

A hidden benefit of sales clubs is the development of long-lasting company and management relationships. Getting away from the office and daily work activities allows for a more relaxed opportunity to get to know your best sales reps in a way that just can't be done during your regular routines.

Employee Recognition Programs

Studies show that companies that frequently recognize their employees greatly outperform other companies. One study found that the top 20 percent of these "recognition rich" companies have a 31 percent lower voluntary turnover rate, a huge measure of performance.[17] Think of how much money CEOs might spend to keep their good people from leaving.

And yet, recognition programs need not be expensive. Recognition can come in the form of gift cards from, say, Starbucks, Amazon, or American Express. Being recognized for successful results, at all levels of the organization, can be very gratifying. One of us still has a personally signed envelope of a $100 gift card that was received early in our career for being the number one rep one month. The personal touch left a powerful, positive impression. Also leaving an impression are the boxes of company pens received for writing up success stories, and a fifteen-dollar Starbucks card that was just someone's way of saying thanks. People like to be recognized. Recognition doesn't even have to be combined with a tangible object; the act of publicly recognizing another person for a job or action well done goes a long way.

---

[17] *The State of Employee Recognition in 2012*, Bersin & Associates

There's no shortage of sources for recognition rewards. The employee recognition industry is estimated to be a forty-five-billion-dollar industry. These recognition companies sell a myriad of gifts, rewards, and incentive programs. Or think about the gift catalogs you receive from Marriott, or Citi's "Thank You" points. Maritz and O.C. Tanner and others have been providing catalogs for years to sales organizations. We used them at several companies. That Weber grill still comes in handy, as do the kitchen pans that came from a recognition contest. If either of us had ever won a Miata or Maserati, you can be sure we'd still be enjoying that, too!

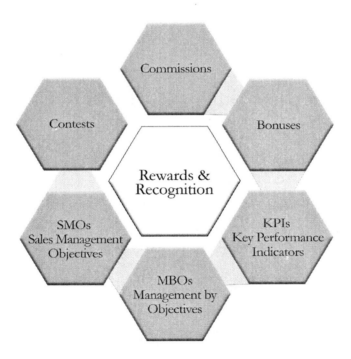

In Our Experience

Some people say sales reps are "coin operated." That's not an expression we've ever particularly cared for, but the truth is that if you want to drive great results, you must develop rewards and recognition plans that drive the right activities, especially in the sales profession!

At one company with a new product launch and a one-year sales cycle, recruiting an "A-team" was essential for putting pilots in place and for accelerating our brand, our differentiated solutions, and our sales cycles. In the first and second quarters, we didn't expect any sales. But by the third quarter, we'd planned to pull in some early adopters. By the fourth quarter, we expected to have a replicable model in place.

To reinforce our desire for these outcomes, and to recruit the "A-team" we developed a quarterly qualitative MBO program. As a team, we set objectives that were stretch goals. If we achieved one-hundred percent of those goals, we could make one-hundred percent of our variable bonus.

We started with objectives that included meeting with a specific number of our ideal customers at the C-level to conduct executive briefings followed by discovery workshops with key, predefined participants. Each quarter, we increased the goals in number and complexity, adding in, for example, a certain number of highly qualified proof of concepts. In the second half, we included sales revenue close targets.

To get operations, finance, and management to approve the approach, the goals had to be lofty with a clear path towards accelerating our go-to-market plans. The MBOs were, in everyone's collective opinion, aggressive. We then added an accelerator to *double* our MBOs (this was the A-team after all!). No one expected us to exceed our stretch goals by double but if you've ever worked with an A-team, you know they stretch, and stretch again. All our top sales achievers took this challenge in stride and expected they would double their compensation. The original stretch goals would yield outstanding results for the company if we met them, and significantly more so if we doubled them.

By recruiting a top-notch team—reps with solid track records, a solid history of results, enthusiastic and passionate—and offering to pay them to be extraordinary, we could select the best of the best. And, we got the results we wanted. In six months, we closed $25 million (100% of our goal) and, after one year, $100 million. In year two, we doubled revenue again. We far exceeded expectations! When the rewards system is aligned with company goals, as it was in this case, then it can drive exceptional sales behavior.

Summary

Opportunities to enhance rewards and recognition include:

- Commission plans that drive the right behavior
- KPIs, SMOs, MBOs to drive specific initiatives
- New account bonuses to emphasize new account wins
- Regular sales or all-hands recognition meetings
- Sales contests to drive specific results
- Annual sales clubs for top performers
- Employee recognition programs

We've experienced several company environments where we can reasonably credit the compensation plan for helping to achieve repeatable and replicable sales results. But it's by no means a certainty. Compensation drives behaviors; this we all know. To drive the *right* sales behaviors, it's necessary to give your reps the *right* incentives.

If your company has a well thought out rewards system, your sales reps will be incented to achieve your company's goals, as well as drive customer delight and retention. Additionally, if the right rewards are put in place, they can drive the result every company desires: MORE sales.

TEN

Enablement

*"Seventy-one percent of companies take more
than six months to get sales reps up to speed."*

CSO INSIGHTS

E nablement is a combination of content and training as well as coaching, mentoring, and onboarding—all designed to help sales reps be successful in their roles. Effective content is so vital to sales success that it necessitates mention in several chapters of this book. It was initially addressed in Chapter 2 ("Messaging") and will be covered in more depth in Chapter 11 ("Essential Sales Tools"). In this chapter, we'll focus on training, coaching, mentoring, and onboarding.

"76% of content marketers are forgetting sales enablement."

HUBSPOT

Training

There are two essential areas of training: product solutions training and sales skills training. In the past, many large technology companies focused on sales training. For example, while working for NCR years ago, we attended the once-famous NCR Sugar Camp Training Center. There was a time when this facility was globally renowned as one of the most modern, state-of-the-art educational facilities in corporate America. In fact, we were required to attend several training courses each year, some of which were several weeks long.

Continuous training and education were integral parts of the culture at NCR. Although today many companies don't train the way they used to, many people still regard companies like NCR, IBM, GE, and Xerox as classic providers of sales training. One big difference between these companies and some of the new high tech organizations is that the sales reps stayed. Did longevity permit more training, or did more training encourage longevity? Regardless, some level of training remains a critical way to differentiate your sales reps and drive MORE sales.

Product or solution training—especially training that focuses on the problem you're solving for your customer—helps your salespeople to be well-armed and successful. Understanding the product or solution is critical. Based on a research firm we spoke with, many of the CIOs they worked with complained that the sales reps didn't understand their own product lines, especially when the product lines were newly introduced.

We've been with companies that had previously not provided formal training for their reps or their channel partners, even though putting together a training program doesn't have to be difficult. Yes, it takes resources, time, and money, but the alternative of sending your sales reps or channel partners into battle unarmed or poorly equipped is a sure recipe for failure.

Some of the training we created internally was with the collective help of sales, marketing, engineering, and operations. Some we outsourced. In general, the focus of the training was exploring answers to such questions as:

- What are the problems customers are facing?

- What is the market? Who are the decision makers?

- What is the solution we offer to solve the problem(s)?

- What is our unique differentiation?

- What are the outcomes this solution can deliver?

- What is our elevator pitch?

- Who is the competition? What are our strengths and weaknesses? What are theirs?

- How do we position ourselves against the competition?

We also focused on common prospect or customer objections and how to overcome them, qualifying questions, proof points, and case studies.

One very effective training tool is role playing. Role playing may seem awkward at first for the participants, but it's always better to practice among peers than in front of a customer.

Pitch contests are another effective way to train. Sales reps and systems engineers (SEs) pair together to record their solution pitches. The pitches can be video recorded for judging and for other sales reps to watch whenever a refresher is needed. In our experience, this has always resulted in good, healthy competition, the result of which is better trained sales reps driving MORE sales.

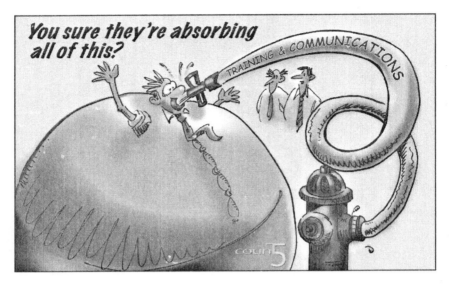

Copyright count5 LLC

What's important is to ensure active learning. Retention naturally drops off over time, but much of what is learned is retained if the learning includes active participation. This is what makes role playing and pitch contests such effective learning methods.

It's important for every sales rep to have sales skills training. It can be through videos, books, or formal training methodologies and courses such as Miller Heiman, Solution Selling, SPIN Selling, Value Selling, Target Account Selling (TAS) (now Altify), the Challenger Sale, as well as many others. By Googling "sales methodologies" you can find a number of the top sales training programs which you can compare.

In addition, outcome-based selling skills are very important in today's marketplace. Courses can be a few hours or weeks, in person or online, integral to weekly, monthly, or quarterly meetings, or ad-hoc. There are a myriad of options. Did you know that millennials (those born between 1984 and 2004), who now make up a high percentage of the workforce, place training and development at the top of their list of worthwhile benefits? Training is critical in recruiting this age group. Be sure to include training as one of the benefits you provide to your sales team. Your company, in turn, will also benefit greatly even if your millennials move on in two or three years; you'll benefit by their short-term increased productivity.

Although we meet sales reps from time to time who feel they're at the top of their games and believe they don't need to attend any additional sales skills training, we know that everyone can sharpen his or her sales techniques. The market is constantly changing and even if it's just one small nugget or gem that your ace salespeople acquire from additional training, it can be invaluable if it enables them to drive MORE sales.

Skills training includes such areas as:

- Selling skills

- Closing skills

- Presentation skills

- White-boarding skills

- Negotiation skills

- Outcome-based selling skills

- Objection handling skills

- Written and verbal communications skills

- Social media skills

All are important. All are worth pursuing.

Coaching and Mentoring

Coaching and mentoring represent another important area of enablement. A high-impact aspect of the job of sales leader is to provide coaching to his or her team. Just as in the sports world, coaches play a significant role in their teams' successes. Ongoing sales coaching from someone who holds a vast amount of experience can be of incredible value to the individuals and to the team. Coached teams achieve 15 percent higher lead conversion rates and 14 percent shorter sales cycles than teams that are not coached.[18] The problem is, only 20 percent of the time spent by sales leaders is spent helping their teams close deals.[19]

Coached teams achieve 15% higher lead conversion rates.

ABERDEEN RESEARCH

And coaching is only going to become more important. Those millenials we mentioned above? Ninety-eight percent surveyed believe working with strong coaches and mentors is an important part of their development.[20]

Onboarding

When a new employee (or channel partner) comes on board, getting them up to speed quickly is important. This might include sales skills- and product solution-based training, but at a minimum must include a clear explanation of internal processes on how to get things done. Many companies, in our experience, leave their newly hired and expensive sales reps to fend for themselves.

Rather than leaving it to chance, try this approach:

- First, get your new employees through all the HR paperwork, set up their laptops, secure their business cards, etc.

---

[18] Aberdeen Research
[19] CSO Insights
[20] "Managing Tomorrow's People: The Future of Work to 2020," PricewaterhouseCoopers, 2008.

- Make sure they fully understand their compensation plan.

- Present them with a clear company overview.

- Acquaint them with the company strategy, mission, and values.

- Make sure they understand the business unit organization chart, i.e., who to go to for help—systems engineers, marketing, support, pricing.

- Make sure they understand their immediate team organization chart.

- Let them know where to find helpful phone lists and emails of other resources within your company.

- Direct them to relevant repositories of information.

- Provide them with the best sales tools—brochures, slide presentations, case studies, etc.

- Make available to them the best internal training courses.

- Make sure they know the sales process and anticipated stages.

- Make sure they understand their pipeline responsibilities.

- Ensure they apply sales funnel reporting discipline so the new sales reps don't inadvertently detract from revenue predictability.

- Educate them on how to configure the solution, the proposal process, how to work with the bid desk, the contract team, and how to place an order.

- Provide them with the dates and times of regularly scheduled meetings.

There is often no shortage of data to share, but make sure you bundle it in a way that's easy to consume. You might include a spreadsheet with dates and milestones. Again, the idea is for your new sales team members to come up to speed quickly and easily.

In Our Experience

To be successful, everyone needs to be trained. Sales teams need to know what the offer is and why it has value to customers. For the teams we've led, we've conducted weekly calls with guest speakers utilizing team-requested presenters and topics. Continuous learning was a key differentiator for our high-performing sales teams. The idea was not to turn the meetings into rote overviews or negative drill downs, but to review areas on which everyone could benefit, where learning was achieved by sharing best practices and ways to overcome challenges in an open brainstorming forum.

We leveraged both internal training resources and outside resources on a regular basis, with both small companies and large. In one case, we also outsourced skills-based training—how to be a more effective sales representative. We focused on basic selling skills, such as research, outreach, prospecting, qualifying, objection handling, attack strategies, and closing tactics. We also trained on major account planning with a focus on defining or creating compelling events.

In one situation, a division turnaround opportunity, sales had been declining. After some investigation we determined that sales training, for both the direct sales force and the channel partners, was woefully inadequate. In fact, it was nonexistent. Consequently, we developed the first-ever direct and channel partner training program in the history of the company. We outsourced our sales skills training, and we used internal resources, systems engineering, marketing, and product marketing to develop and deliver our solution training.

We conducted the internal direct sales training first, to work out any kinks. The following week we brought in all of the channel partners. In addition to training them, bringing them in allowed us to deepen our relationships with them. In the end, we turned a team with slumping sales numbers into a team that beat their target within the next six months!

Everyone in sales who wants to meet and exceed their quotas, at the same time earning a lot of commission dollars, wants to know how to sell MORE, and how do to so quickly and effectively. While some sales reps may complain about having to do training, from our experience we can confirm that a single new idea or technique learned in training, or from being coached or mentored, can yield significant sales results along with corresponding commissions. To be at the top of one's game, you need to stay sharp.

Summary

Improving enablement can include:

- Solution training

- Skills training

- Coaching and mentoring

- Onboarding

Training is essential. There's not a company in business that can't benefit by enhancing the sales skills of its employees. Even a veteran salesperson typically gleans at least one nugget from training that will benefit his or her sales efforts. In addition to skills training, solution training is vital. Since every company is different, new hires typically need in-depth solution training. And everyone needs training when new offers are released. Most sales reps don't become experts by reading their company website, or reading product brochures. Sales enablement, including solutions and sales skills training, coaching and mentoring, and onboarding, is crucial to driving MORE sales.

In the next chapter, we'll review essential sales tools. Properly designed and communicated, sales tools provide sales reps ready access to and reinforcement of the key areas on which they have been trained.

ELEVEN

Essential Sales Tools

"Sixty percent of sales leaders find that lack of proper tools lengthens sales cycles."

CSO Insights

Sales tools are many and varied and can generally be categorized as:

1   Software sales tools

2   External sales tools

3   Internal sales tools

We'll briefly cover the first two and focus more on the third, but it's important to recognize that each tool can be an essential key to success in driving MORE sales.

Software Sales Tools

There are many software selling tools and plugins available from a wide variety of vendors. These software tools help to make sales more efficient, consistent, and predictable. In most cases, it makes sense to leverage third-party tools rather than invent them yourself. Customer Relationship Management (CRM) tools, for example, are readily available from many vendors. With simple customization, they can be easily adapted to align with your company's terminology and sales processes. With today's flexible licensing and pricing options, for those systems, there's no need to recreate the wheel. Leveraging a tool that is well known in the industry can expedite implementation, shorten training time, and increase adoption rates significantly.

Some of the categories of sales tools that are available include:

- Customer Relationship Management (CRM)

- Account planning and management

- Capabilities development and measurement

- Compensation, quota, and territory

- Configure, Price, Quote (CPQ) and contract management

- Gamification

- Sales development

- Lead and database management

- Opportunity management

- Performance management and coaching

- Pipeline management and deal flow

- Prospect and customer engagement

- Sales enablement

- Value selling and ROI

Bottom line: there are a *lot* of software sales tools and new ones are coming into play all the time. Staying informed about all the options can be a daunting task. Nancy Nardin, CEO of Smart Selling Tools[21] provides a repository for selling tools and offers a "Top Sales Tools" guide. It's an excellent resource to get a quick handle on many of the options available. To start, think about which sales challenges you need to solve and in what priority. Then, you can begin investigating what might be the best software tool for you.

External Sales Tools

External sales tools are called that because they are customer-facing (including channel-partner-facing). These tools are usually created by marketing and are intended for use with customers. External sales tools can include:

- Company brochures

- Product and solution data sheets

- Case studies

- Whitepapers

- Slide presentations

- Websites

- Newsletters

- Videos

- Webinars

---

[21] *www.smartsellingtools.com*

- Reference lists

- Calculators—Return on Investment (ROI) or Total Cost of Ownership (TCO)

Internal Sales Tools

Internal sales tools are typically *not* presented directly to a customer; rather, they are used by salespeople as part of the sales process to increase the probability of winning, to shorten the overall time to close, or to increase the size of the deal.

One effective way for sales reps to be more successful is to create and share great content and then package it in the form of internal sales tools that other salespeople can leverage. This also helps sales teams practice what they learned in their training events, understand how they won a big deal, and share with their peers their personal best practices. All of this helps create repeatable results.

It may be surprising to learn that 55 percent of sales content is created by sales teams rather than marketing.[22] Some of the best internal sales tools include:

- Success stories

- Battle cards

- Qualifying questions

- Sales playbooks

- Sales "scripts" for email and voicemail

- Elevator pitches

- Use Cases

---

[22] CSO Insights

- Competitive assessments and SWOT analyses

- Account plans

- Proposal templates

- Sales guides

Let's look at a few of these in more detail.

Success Stories

Everyone likes a good story. We discussed the need for great stories in the chapter on Rewards and Recognition. A well-told story can be both highly effective and easy to remember. Customer references make great stories and prospects appreciate hearing about companies in their industry that had similar problems and how those problems were solved. Success stories (also known as case studies or use cases) are very useful for enabling sales to communicate success to prospects in similar companies and industries.

Components of a success story should include:

- The name of the company

- The industry

- The problem the customer was having

- Your solution

- Quantitative results (e.g., outcomes achieved, ROI, percent increase in sales, reduced time to market, etc.)

- Who the competition was

- How and why you won

The logos from these companies can be valuable on your website, your presentations, in conversations, in your elevator pitch, and in your press releases. (Of course, to make use of a logo you'll need the company's release and approval.) Be careful that your success stories don't reveal pricing, competitive secrets—or weaknesses.

See Chapter 2 on messaging for more information on developing an effective elevator pitch. Elevator pitches are crucial, especially in an era when multiple resources provide lead generation and multiple follow-up calls are required!

Battle Cards

Battle cards are compelling documents that provide sales teams with impactful and highly relevant information in a nutshell. They're typically created as a joint effort between marketing and sales. Battle cards highlight whom to sell to and how to best position your solutions. A battle card might include such material as:

- Your tag line

- Your elevator pitch

- Any industry accolades (e.g., Gartner, Forbes, etc.)

- Your unique differentiation

- The target market

- Your ideal customer profile

- Your competition's strengths and weaknesses

- Qualifying questions

We're advocates of one-page battle cards to keep it simple and useable, but two-page battle cards can also be effective. Any more than two pages can turn readers off. The one- or two-page battle card can be easily posted on the wall in one's office or cubicle and it's also easy to glance at on your tablet, smart phone, or notebook during a meeting. Less is typically best, but whatever you can fit onto two pages is okay to include.

Qualifying Questions

In Chapter 5, Optimized Sales Processes, we covered the importance of moving your opportunities forward through the sales pipeline by continuously qualifying your prospects. And the best way is to ask the right questions. An invaluable sales tool is a list of qualifying questions. It's worth reviewing the list from Chapter 5:

- What is the business problem you are trying to solve?

- Who all is involved in making the decision?

- What is the decision process?

- What is your timeline for having a solution in place?

- Is there a compelling event? Is the project already in your budget? Can you share what that is?

- Is there an incumbent? Can you describe what was working? Not working? Why are you making a change?

- What are the decision criteria for this opportunity? What are the key criteria management typically uses to measure success?

Sales Playbooks

Particularly for new hires, a sales playbook can be incredibly helpful. A sales playbook is basically a set of plays to help your sales reps succeed in selling your offering. It's their go-to handbook with all the how-to recipes needed to win. Information to include in your sales playbook:

Company Information

- Overview of the company

- The team charter and goals

- The sale stages, and what is minimally required at each stage (with consistent terminology)

- Responsibilities of the sales team, the supporting teams, and relevant partners

- Clearly-defined roles and responsibilities (sometimes referred to as swim lanes) and contact information on key resources

- Where to find information on any topic (such as a link or person)

Messaging and Offerings

- Your elevator pitch

- Solution overviews

- Specific offers and services

- Special promotions

Target Prospects

- An "ideal client" profile

- The target market and target titles

Sales Tools

- Sales tools available—the links, the training, the experts

- Qualifying questions

- A call plan and preparation

- Competition—strengths and weaknesses
- Information on learning about prospects, industry, and trends; how to research using online research tools

Be careful with your sales playbook; you want it to get read, you want it to be referred to, and you want it to result in more sales. You don't want something that's going to be thumped down on someone's desk, something that will be overwhelming, hard to consume, or, worse, ignored. Be sure it's crisp, and if you can keep each section to a single or a few pages, it will be easier to read and understand. Whenever possible, make it visual and intuitive. And most importantly, keep it updated!

In Our Experience

Sales tools can be an incredibly powerful and impactful way to drive MORE sales. They're not one-time events; they must be kept current based on changes in your own offerings, your market, or your competition. And to be especially effective, they need to be informative and easy to use. We once developed sales tools for a reseller channel partner that were so effective, our own internal sales teams used them, too. In fact, we won several awards that year for best sales tools and best information products. Our secret? We made the tools crisp, concise, compelling, and graphically eye-catching.

With battle cards we've used them both internally and with our reseller/channel partners. Partners typically don't have as much bandwidth dedicated towards your offerings as your own sales teams. For us, having compelling one- or two-page battle cards allowed us to put the absolute best sales tools in the hands of all of our partners.

We've encountered many sales teams over the years that said they weren't getting what they needed to be successful from marketing. There was often inconsistent messaging or poor collateral.

Our perspective has always been that if we own the quota, and our jobs are the ones on the line, then we need to be clear about asking for the proper tools or creating them ourselves. After all, if you're going to battle, you need tools that work. No doubt you have formidable competitors. Arm your sales teams with the tools that help them position your offerings better than the competition. Put your salespeople in the best position to win.

Summary

Leverage essential sales tools to drive MORE sales. Sales tools can include:

- Software sales tools

- External sales tools

- Internal sales tools including

  - Success stories

  - Battle cards

  - Qualifying questions

  - Sales playbooks

There are many sales tools options to assist your sales reps. The key isn't quantity, but quality. Essential sales tools are ones that can be used over and over. They should be proven, battle tested, and derived from best practices. Having easy-to-use software sales tools enables your sales teams to be more effective in the sales process. Leveraging external sales tools, typically in the form of marketing collateral, provides consistency in your messaging to prospects from all members of your customer-facing teams. Internal sales tools provide selling tips and tricks that enable your sales teams to drive more sales. When used properly, these essential sales tools can help shorten the sales cycle, increase win and close rates, and drive a more replicable model for *all* your salespeople and channel partners.

Sales tools are vital to a salesperson's success. They'll help you and your teams to drive MORE sales. Make them a priority!

TWELVE

Execution

"Without execution, strategy is useless."

Morris Chang, CEO of TSMC

You can develop an outstanding, well-thought-out sales plan. You can have the most researched sales processes in the world. Your strategy approach and messaging can be battle-tested, targeted at a well understood market with market-competitive prices, and better than all your competitors. Still, your sales teams will fail without *proper execution*. (And all the information you've learned thus far in this book will go to waste!)

© 1999 Ted Goff

"Our study concludes that this is the percentage of our customers who will buy from us without any effort whatsoever on our part."

Consider these revealing facts:

"In 2007, it took an average of 3.68 cold call attempts to reach a prospect. Today, it takes 8 attempts."

TELENET & OVATION SALES GROUP

"The average salesperson only makes 2 attempts to reach a prospect."

SIRIUS DECISIONS

"80% of sales require 5 follow-up phone calls after the initial meeting."

THE MARKETING DONUT

"44% of salespeople give up after 1 follow-up call."

THE MARKETING DONUT

Having a plan is not enough. To have repeatable and replicable wins, sales teams must work the plan in a diligent and focused fashion.

"Good ideas are common – what's uncommon are people who will work hard enough to bring them about."

ASHLEIGH BRILLIANT

Own Your Success: Accountability and Dashboards

When it comes to your sales team's performance, are you able to answer these questions: Are your sales reps identifying enough business opportunities to be successful? Is the velocity of recent activity (30–90 days) sufficient? Are projects taking too long to close? What is the win/loss rate?

Some sales reps believe that customer relationship management (CRM) is just a tool management uses to scrutinize them. But sales reps and management who understand that CRM is an effective way to help salespeople drive more sales are more successful than those who don't understand this. They also realize that it's a great tool to track progress.

Another especially beneficial tool for individuals, teams, and management are dashboards. Dashboards help improve personal sales productivity and improve focus. CRM administrators or operations typically create the dashboards based on metrics that sales management wants to track. Dashboards can utilize text or graphs to depict the numbers. A quick view of your weekly pipeline, 30 days, the quarter, and Q+1 (current quarter plus one quarter out) can be highly informative. Dashboards can also show your top five or ten deals and identify the pipeline stage they're in. A dashboard can also be configured to show percentage of quota on an individual or team basis. That way it's possible to project if you have enough pipeline to make your quota, and you can course-correct if you find that you're coming up short.

Sales and Account Plans

Sales organizations with a defined account planning process are 41% more likely to meet and exceed revenue targets.

Because you are more likely to win business from an existing customer than a new one, account planning is a proven strategy for achieving predictable revenue growth.

And not only is the win rate higher, but the sales cycle is shorter and the deal sizes are larger.

"INSIDE THE BUYER'S MIND":
THE ALTIFY BUYER/SELLER VALUE INDEX 2016, ALTIFY FOUNDATION

Account plans are crucial for key accounts. So is territory planning if you have a large geography-based territory with numerous accounts. Proper sales execution demands that you actively manage the plan. Focus areas should include the action, owner, and timeline.

Sales/account plans include things such as:

- Customer

- Top Customer Initiatives

- Customer Spend/Current Solutions

- White Space

- Decision Makers

- Executive Mapping
- SWOT
- Competitive Vendors
- Current Pipeline
- Expansion Opportunities
- New Pipeline
- Actions and Owners

At several of the companies where we worked, we conducted facilitated sessions for our largest customers. Not only were those accounts strategic to us, we were strategic to them. We asked the customer to send a representative to us at the beginning of the session to present to us an overview of their organization, their top initiatives, and where they needed help. A brainstorming session, with typically just the internal stakeholders (sales, solutions engineers, service, specialists, management, etc.), followed. We would list the customer's top initiatives and then map our solutions to them. At the end of the session we had a new pipeline, and a new plan on how to go after the new opportunities.

Getting teams together to collaborate and brainstorm brings a lot of new and fresh thinking. Further, it provides a way to get all the resources aligned to meet common goals (more sales and delighted customers). We always looked for new opportunities to solve our customer's problems and meet their desired outcomes.

Territory plans are important in managing territories. Content might include:

- Geography
- Historical Spend

- Current Vendors/Incumbents

- Prospecting Tactics

- Existing Accounts

- TAM (Total Addressable Market)

- Competition

- List of Prospective Accounts

- Current Pipeline

- Demand Generation

- What Assistance is Needed

- Actions/Owners

Sales Reviews

Reviews should be held on a recurring schedule, on either the account level or the territory level. You can't write a plan and put it in a drawer. You need to work it: execute and show progress on a regular basis. At most companies where we've worked, reviews were done at least quarterly.

Sales reviews are often best conducted face to face, although in some situations phone discussions are better than nothing. We found it best for sales management to physically meet with the sales teams at least half the time. That provides more quality time for building relationships with the team before and after the sales reviews.

Sales reps that create sales plans have a higher probability of success. Plans help them navigate, set goals, and put the actions in place to achieve those goals.

Weekly Forecast Reviews

To the typical sales rep, manager, VP, or even SVP of sales, weekly forecast reviews may seem excessive. But if the reviews provide useful information both ways, the process can be valuable. Since making your numbers is a top priority, forecast reviews ensure a focused view of progress and a means by which timely assistance can be provided.

These weekly data-collection opportunities are often attended by an operations person to help gather and circulate the numbers shared. In all cases, however, it's important for sales management to attend, to be sure everyone values the time spent on this important step.

Inspect what you expect.

ANONYMOUS

There is good execution, and there is over inspection. In Chapter 4 on operations, we shared a quote from Jack Welch that referenced the idea that only 30 to 35 percent of a salesperson's face time is spent with the customer. Clearly the amount of time not spent on customers is ineffective. Be sure that your internal processes and reviews provide valuable contributions to the success of your sales reps and to your business.

Inspection and Cadence

Although execution in sales is often thought of as an individual effort, it's also a team effort. Consequently, the leader of the sales team plays a vital role in ensuring the team is executing and meeting business objectives. One way to accomplish this is through inspection. If you're constantly watching your metrics—as an individual, a team, and as a leader—you make it known that results are an important part of the company culture.

Additionally, there needs to be a regular cadence around inspection. In our experience, mentioned earlier and worth mentioning again, a best practice is four funnel reviews each week (depending on the number of levels in your company):

1   Sales rep to manager. One-on-one between each sales rep and his or her sales manager. Dashboards can be created to track pipeline by individual sales rep. The goal is for sales reps to take personal accountability for their pipeline, but weekly reviews also ensure focus and provide support where needed. Sales management is in the "no surprises" business. They don't want surprises from the reps and they don't want their executive management to be surprised.

2   Region sales. Team funnel reviews between the sales leaders (directors or VPs) and their sales managers. In this review, sales managers discuss their team's forecast and any gaps with their peers and direct leaders.

3   Global Sales. These are company funnel reviews between the executive sales team (by geography, for example, or, in a smaller company, across the organization). These reviews are attended by the sales leaders and the sales executives of the company or division to present the current forecast view and areas of opportunity to be pursued during that week.

4   Corporate. This is a rollup at the end of the week. This review consolidates all the input and what will be rolled up for the entire team to be presented in the next executive management review.

It's important to review the current period in detail. But in addition to the current period, it's critical to also review the next period. Minimally (depending on your business, sales cycles, close rates, etc.), you should look at your pipeline on a Q+1 (current plus next quarter) basis, so that you don't end a quarter on a high note due to intense focus, only to find that you completely overlooked generating pipeline for the next quarter. Starting a quarter flat-footed can put you in a difficult spot.

You may also consider looking at your CRM pipeline with a full one year projected. How big should your pipeline be in terms of dollar value versus annual quota? Five to one? More? Less? See Chapter 3 on Metrics for an example on calculating what's needed in the pipeline, based on quota, average selling price, and close rate.

Bid Desk (Big Deal) Reviews

All deals over a certain size should be reviewed with specified members of the executive staff. These reviews can be scheduled for a specific day each week with the objective being either general awareness or to accomplish a specific action, such as a request for better pricing, or involvement from a key resource.

The executive staff review should also ensure that executives are aligned across the organization to assist in closing the deal either by getting personally involved or via resources they can provide from other organizations to assist.

Close Plan Reviews

Making your forecast, of course, means closing your opportunities. In several companies, we conducted weekly "close reviews" on predetermined accounts. These sessions were designed not to be interrogations, but rather opportunities for several sales reps, their management, and the VP to review the largest opportunities in the pipeline for that quarter in a collaborative fashion to yield better results.

Items that can be covered and tracked in weekly close reviews might include (see also pages 64 and 65):

- The solution offered and competition

- Key contacts, economic buyers, decision makers, influencers, approvers, etc.

- The critical dates—RFP, contract expiration date, implementation date, etc.

- The compelling event; i.e., what's compelling the customer to act by the date in question: Contract expiration? Strategic imperative? Launch date? Other?

- Risks and risk mitigation

- Activity—what needs to be done, by whom, and by when?
    - What is the next action to get the order?
    - What does the sales rep need from anyone else in the firm to get the order?

It's important to utilize common language about the status of a project. When you say it's "closed" or it's "won," what does that mean? For example, did you get the full order this month or a partial order? What portion of the order will hit the company's books, and when? Some orders are scheduled over time, or delayed. Perhaps there was only a verbal commit, or the project is on hold. "Closed" could also refer to "lost"! When it comes to the words being used to describe a project's status, make sure management and reps are all on the same page.

For us, the key to these meetings was in looking for gaps, next steps, actions, owners, and dates. Another benefit was the opportunity for everybody to share their experiences and offer their best ideas. Sales reps enjoyed sharing their progress and learning about similar situations from their peers and management. The reviews also gave management an opportunity to allocate needed resources. Close plan reviews yielded higher close rates due to a very focused, detailed collaborative set of actions.

> *By constant practices, deliberate repetitions*
> *and uninterrupted exercises, leaders go*
> *from zero to hero. They don't quit.*

ISRAELMORE AYIVOR

The objective is for every player on the team to take an active role in helping to drive MORE sales. We've been on teams where it took a wide range of resources at many levels to complete a win. Winning at sales is a team sport where everyone on the team needs to execute with passion.

Summary

> *"A goal without a plan is just a wish."*

ANTOINE DE SAINT-EXUPÉRY

> *"If you don't know where you are going,*
> *you'll end up someplace else."*

YOGI BERRA

The key to driving MORE sales and meeting or exceeding objectives is execution.

Execution includes, but is not limited to:

- Owning your success—accountability and dashboards
- Sales and account plans

- Sales reviews
- Weekly forecast reviews
- Inspection and cadence
- Bid desk (big deal reviews)
- Close plan reviews

There is a lot of effort that goes into building successful sales organizations. There are many ideas, many game plans for success. It's an intense focus on execution of the actions that sets the successful sales reps and sales teams apart from the rest. Winners focus on executing their plans!

THIRTEEN

Summing it All Up

When we set out to write a book based on our MORE Sales Framework, the goal was to convey ideas that were researched, tested, and used. Nothing you've read in this book is merely theoretical. We were part of organizations ranging from small start-up companies to large multinational corporations that implemented the principles discussed in these chapters and with extraordinary success.

Before we summarize what you've read so far, there are two additional aspects to the MORE Sales Framework that you may have noticed throughout this book. These threads matrix across all the other elements and are worth emphasizing explicitly here. They are the glue that holds the MORE Sales Framework together, ensuring your ongoing success:

- Aligned teamwork

- Continuous improvement

Aligned Teamwork

Repeatable, replicable sales results is the key to the success of sales and sales management. How can you replicate success? How can you package up what's working and turn it into a repeatable sales process?

The linchpin is to get your team working *as a team*. Learn—together—what works and what doesn't. Incent your team to share their experiences. Emphasize communication. Everyone on the sales team benefits by sharing with their peers their successes and failures. Understanding, team-wide, what works and what doesn't will help each team member's approach and shorten everyone's sales cycle. Repeatable processes result in maximized results.

©Glasbergen
glasbergen.com

"There is no 'I' in 'TEAM' unless you turn off your spell-checker."

Observing the true trends in your win and loss analysis has the highest impact when done as a team. This works effectively as a cross-functional effort, also. Why are you losing? Why are you winning? Track it in your CRM, and ensure that someone in your company is diligently taking the feedback for improvements. This information should be shared with sales, marketing, product engineering, services, as well as other interested internal parties.

It's not always easy to accomplish, but aligning sales and marketing is a must. Unfortunately, misalignment is a common issue at many companies and you saw it referenced in several chapters of this book. As we've discussed, alignment between these two essential organizational entities can have a profound impact on your results, from close ratio, to better performing sales reps, to higher revenues.

Always remember that sales is a team sport. You may have heard that for some offerings it takes a full-court press to win a deal. There's no question that for driving MORE sales, teamwork and alignment are essential.

Continuous Improvement

In addition to sharing and replicating a model that works, never stop looking for better ways. Sales can never be a 100-percent cookie-cutter approach; there is always a need for tweaks, opportunities for improvement, and, sometimes, even a complete overhaul.

Offerings change and are updated, markets and prospects shift, and competitors get stronger. Today's winning strategies won't remain winning strategies forever. Constantly look for new ways in which to improve your market penetration, improve your messaging, and make your metrics more meaningful. Look for new ways to offload more of the non-selling tasks to operations, optimize your processes, and make sure you're meeting the changing needs and desired outcomes of your customers. Stay on top of winning approaches with channel partners, recognition and rewards, and retention and referrals. And always look for ways to provide better enablement, more impactful essential sales tools, and greater execution of your sales plan.

Watching your competitors, staying on top of macro and niche market and technology trends, staying in tune with best practices, trying new and improved methodologies—these are all ways to keep getting better. Your efforts to continuously improve, across all the elements of the MORE Sales Framework, combined with proper alignment across your entire organization, will set the stage for extraordinary results.

Summing up the Elements of the MORE Sales Framework

The MORE Sales Framework begins with knowing your **market**. New offerings fail every day because the right market for the offering goes unidentified. Use the principles we've learned to refine your market definition.

Consider your **messaging** and all the ways in which your offering is made known to your prospects. Are you employing a What's In It For Me strategy or a What's In It For Them strategy? What's your elevator pitch? Remember to have a clear message that resonates with the audience and solves a customer's problem, achieves their goals, delivers outcomes, or eliminates or reduces an unnecessary hurdle.

To manage your business proactively, know your **metrics**. *What gets measured gets done.* Focus on your sales opportunity pipeline, work to increase your close rates and expand your average selling price.

Imperative for your success is having a top-notch **operations** team that can take the administrative burden off of your sales organization. Processing orders, revenue recognition, ensuring contracts are balanced—none of these are areas that can be compromised.

Optimized sales processes can significantly improve the efficiency of working with your prospects and converting them to happy customers. Refine each stage in the selling process to more quickly move your prospect to the close.

To create exceptional customer experiences in today's selling environment, you'll want to utilize **outcome-based selling**. Being focused on the customer's outcomes and solving their business problems is the catalyst for building a successful business and long-lasting relationships.

Resellers and channel partners can rapidly and significantly expand your brand and your market coverage, putting more feet on the street and thus developing more sales reps to tout your solution. The key is enabling them and giving them the resources to be successful.

Retention and referrals represent an invaluable way to maintain and grow your company. There's simply no substitute for providing superior service. Focus on feedback, create loyalty programs, and actively seek referral business. This is important to your success in a competitive marketplace.

Remember that properly motivating and propelling your sales organization requires **rewards and recognition**. Commission plans that drive the right behavior, bonuses, recognition meetings, and sales contests are just some of the ways that you can motivate your sales reps and your channel partners to achieve your company's goals of meeting sales objectives and achieving customer delight.

Also necessary is the continued improvement of your sales organization. **Enablement** of your sales and channel partner reps includes ongoing training and mentoring. There's not a company in business that can't benefit by enhancing the sales skills of its sales reps.

To do so, also means providing them with **essential sales tools**. Whether it's sales scripts, success stories, account plans, or playbooks, essential sales tools are ones that can be easily used over and over. They should be proven, battle-tested, and derived from observing what works.

Finally, it comes down to **execution**. There are many game plans for success but it's the successful execution of the necessary and desired actions that sets the successful sales team apart from the rest. Excellence in execution requires constant planning and regular reviews.

We know—through real-world experience—that when a company intentionally and systematically works on and applies the 12 elements of the MORE Sales Framework, their sales will increase. We wish you great success in driving MORE sales!

M.O.R.E. Sales Framework ™

M	O	R	E
•Market	•Operations	•Resellers	•Enablement
•Messaging	•Optimized Processes	•Retention & Referrals	•Essential Sales Tools
•Metrics	•Outcomes	•Rewards & Recognition	•Execution

Teamwork, Alignment, Continuous Improvement

Glossary of Acronyms

ABP: Account Business Plan

ARR: Annual Recurring Revenue

ASP: Average Selling Price

B2B: Business to Business

B2C: Business to Consumer

CAB: Customer Advisory Board

CAC: Customer Acquisition Cost

CAM: Customer Account Manager

CM: Contribution Margin

CPQ: Configure, Price, Quote

CRM: Customer Relationship Management

CSM: Customer Success Manager

CSAT: Customer Satisfaction

CSP: Cloud Service Provider

ERP: Enterprise Resource Planning

FFYR: First Fiscal Year Revenue

GTM: Go-to-Market

IaaS: Infrastructure as a Service

ICP: Ideal Customer Profile

IT: Information Technology

IDC: International Data Corporation

KPI: Key Performance Indicator

LCV: Lifetime Customer Value

LTV: Lifetime Value

MBO: Management by Objective

MDR: Market Development Representative

MoM: Month over Month

MQL: Marketing Qualified Lead

MRR: Monthly Recurring Revenue

MSP: Managed Service Provider

MTD: Month to Date

NPS: Net Promoter Score

OEM: Original Equipment Manufacturer

PaaS: Platform as a Service

POC: Proof of Concept

PRM: Partner Relationship Management

Q+1: Quarter plus One

QBR: Quarterly Business Review

QTD: Quarter to Date

RFP: Request for Proposal

ROI: Return on Investment

SaaS: Software as a Service

SDK: Software Development Kit

SDR: Sales Development Representative

SE: Systems Engineer or Solutions Engineer

SG&A: Sales, General and Administrative Expenses

SI: Systems Integrator

SLA: Service Level Agreement

SMB: Small Medium Business

SMO: Sales Management Objective

SOW: Statement of Work

SP: Solutions Provider

SPIF: Sales Performance Incentive Fund

SQL: Sales Qualified Lead

SWOT: Strengths, Weaknesses, Opportunities, Threats

TAM: Total Addressable Market

TAS : Target Account Selling

TCO: Total Cost of Ownership

VAR: Value Added Reseller

TCV: Total Contract Value

WIIFM: What's In It For Me?

WIIFT: What's In It For Them?

WTD: Week to Date

YoY: Year over Year

YTD: Year to Date

Acknowledgments

We would like to thank all the renowned experts who assisted us by contributing to this book. Special gratitude goes to the individuals below. Your knowledge and expertise helped make this book a reality. Thank you all!

Erna Arnesen

Chief Channel and Alliances Officer
Vice President Alliances, Channel Sales and Marketing
Symantec, Cisco, Plantronics, Apple, NeXT, ZL Technologies

Bob Bacon

Vice President Global Sales Operations
Operations / Compensation / Enablement

Randy Bell

Vice President at HP, Dell and NCR
CEO at Nanotechnologies

Joanne S. Black

Founder, No More Cold Calling®
Published Author of Two Top Sales Books
Lead Generation and Referral Selling Expert

Stephen Denny

Author, Killing Giants: 10 Strategies to Topple the Goliath In Your Industry (Portfolio, 2011) | Keynote Speaker
Managing Director at Denny Leinberger Strategy LLC & President of Denny Marketing | Global Trend Research and Marketing Consulting

Jonelle Gilden

CEO, JGilden Consulting, LLC

Sales Training Performance Consultant, Facilitator, Instructional Designer, Writer and Master Trainer

Fred Kendall

Managing Director

Hogarth & Ogilvy (a WPP owned agency)

Ralph Lentz

Executive Vice President of Sales and Customer Success

Presence Learning, Macrovision, Computer Associates

Gary Mendel

Vice President, Global Sales

Spire Global, Wandisco, Macromedia, AT&T

Nancy Nardin

CEO, Founder of Smart Selling Tools

Expert on Sales Technology to Drive Revenue

Jim O'Gara

COO, SVP, Sales and Alliances

BDS Mobile, SugarCRM, FrontRange, Apple

John O'Leary

Vice President of Sales, Marketing and Strategic Partnerships

Digital Guardian, Code Green Networks

Susan Rabi

Vice President, CFO, Global Sales and Marketing, Planning and Operations, Business Process Improvement, Continuous Improvement

NCR and HP

Scott Schafer

Executive VP, SVP and VP, Sales, Marketing and Services
Arecont Vision, Schneider Electric/Pelco, Reynolds and
Reynolds, NCR

Kathie Sherman

President, TenFour Marketing, Inc.
Direct Marketing – Response Doubler
Former President Women in Consulting

Deb Siegle

President, Strategic Marketing Solutions – Strategist and Market
Researcher
Named one of Silicon Valley's Top Women of Influence
U of M School of Information Entrepreneurship Advisory
Committee, former President Women in Consulting, Women in
Telecom

Arnab Sur

Sr. Vice President, Sales, Chief Revenue Officer
ServiceNow, Qooco, AT&T

Tom Webster

CEO and President, TONE
Chief Marketing Officer, VP of Marketing
PSC, Wire One, Teradata

And special thanks to an incredible mentor:

Ernie von Simson

President, Ostriker von Simson, Inc.
Senior Partner (Ret.), The Research Board
Senior Partner (Ret.), CIO Strategy Exchange (CIOSE)

For MORE information on Driving MORE Sales,
please visit *www.Driving-More-Sales.com*

What Executives Are Saying about
Driving More Sales: 12 Essential Elements

"CEOs: pay attention!! Driving More Sales hands you the keys to the sales "black box" and provides the steering wheel needed to accelerate sales growth. It is jam packed with practical insight that will help your company today!"

MIKE RUFFOLO
CHAIRMAN, EDGEWARE AB
FORMER CEO – INTERNAP CORPORATION, CROSSBEAM SYSTEMS AND LIQUID
MACHINES

"One recurrent problem I've observed while serving on boards of directors is the lack of effective communications regarding sales strategies and tactics among C-suite executives. Watkins and Doster have provided a sophisticated set of benchmarks and best practices to drive this vital dialogue."

ERNIE VON SIMSON
PRESIDENT, OSTRIKER VON SIMSON, INC.
SENIOR PARTNER, CIO STRATEGY EXCHANGE (RETIRED)

"Outstanding execution is going to make the difference in delivering impressive sales results. Readers who embrace the processes outlined in this book, and make them a part of what they do every day, week, month, and quarter will be better positioned for success. This is not just a guide for sales management; it is imperative that all senior management be aligned to the sales process."

SCOTT SCHAFER
EXECUTIVE VICE PRESIDENT, SALES, MARKETING AND SERVICES
ARECONT VISION

"All executives want more sales. These timeless top-line-growth insights will challenge you in your pursuit of success. And, who doesn't want to read a workbook for winning?"

ERIC ROEGNER
EXECUTIVE VICE PRESIDENT,
GROUP PRESIDENT, ROLLED PRODUCTS, ARCONIC

"In banking, as in the tech industry, a well-researched path to winning in sales makes the difference in achieving your company and personal goals."

JOHNNY PASSYN
SENIOR VICE PRESIDENT, PERFORMANCE MANAGEMENT
US BANKING SECTOR

Driving MORE Sales
12 Essential Elements